FLIPPING PROPERTIES

Generate Instant Cash Profits in Real Estate

William Bronchick
Robert Dahlstrom

Dearborn™
Trade Publishing
A **Kaplan Professional** Company

Vice President and Publisher: Cynthia A. Zigmund
Editorial Director: Donald J. Hull
Acquisitions Editor: Mary B. Good
Senior Project Editor: Trey Thoelcke
Interior Design: Lucy Jenkins
Cover Design: Scott Rattray Design
Typesetting: the dotted i

Printed in the United States of America
02 03 10 9 8 7 6 5

Library of Congress Cataloging-in-Publication Data

Bronchick, William.
   Flipping properties : generate instant cash profits in real estate / William Bronchick, Robert Dahlstrom.
       p.   cm.
   Includes index.
   ISBN 0-7931-4491-4 (pbk.)
   1. Real estate investment. 2. House buying 3. House selling. 4. Real estate business. I. Dahlstrom, Robert, 1962- . II. Title.
HD1382.5 .B755 2001
332.63'24—dc21

                                                                                      2001001424

Contents

Introduction

Real estate has probably made more millionaires than any other financial vehicle. A full-time or part-time venture into real estate investing offers many financial and personal rewards, including cash flow, security, and long-term wealth. There are many ways to profit in real estate; the question is, which method is right for you?

THE TRADITIONAL APPROACH TO REAL ESTATE INVESTING

The traditional concept of real estate investment requires one to invest money, then wait for something to happen. Typically, people buy real estate for income and appreciation. They expect that after 30 years or so, their mortgages will be paid off and they will receive a generous cash flow for their retirement years. These assumptions are generally correct, and many people have become wealthy by owning rental real estate. Rental properties continue to be an excellent vehicle for creating long-term wealth and income for retirement. However, acquiring and managing rental properties requires cash for down payments, credit to obtain financing, and time to deal with tenants. We do not discourage owning rental properties, but rather suggest that you get some experience and working capital before venturing into rentals.

THE SPECULATOR'S APPROACH

Some investors are speculators, that is, they buy property they expect will go up in value, creating a good return on the capital invested. This increase in value depends largely on outside factors, such as rezoning, surrounding developments, and market inflation. Although many people have made millions of dollars on real estate speculations, just as many have gone bankrupt. Thus, speculation is a large gamble, and not well suited for inexperienced investors.

THE "NOTHING DOWN" APPROACH

"Nothing down" is another concept in the real estate world. Many beginning investors are lured to real estate by the late-night television gurus who showcase their millionaire students who bought real estate with no money. Beware, many of these people are paid actors, and some are just plain lucky. Investing no money in real estate usually means that most of the funds for the acquisition price are borrowed. Highly leveraged real estate purchases (borrowing most of the money to purchase real estate) can often lead to negative cash flow when vacancies arise or when repairs or even routine maintenance is required. The people you don't see are the ones who bought properties with no money down and who have no cash reserves for the difficult times. Case in point:

Tens of thousands of highly leveraged investors lost all their properties in the real estate crash of the late 1980s.

Not all gurus are frauds nor is buying real estate with nothing down always a bad idea. Just be wary of exaggerated claims that real estate investing is a fast or easy way to get rich.

THE WAY THINGS ARE IN THE REAL WORLD

The reality is that real estate is like any other business—you don't get rich overnight, it takes hard work and time to accumulate wealth. In fact, most start-up companies actually lose money their first year or two in business. The companies that survive past the first few years, however, often become profitable and continue to grow. While it is possible to make money right away in your real estate business, you may not see a substantial profit for several years.

Because most businesses fail in the early years from lack of cash flow, we recommend that you generate working capital before you buy properties that are keepers. Certainly, you can buy properties with little or no money down, but you will need cash reserves to get you through the difficult times that every investor encounters. While a comfortable retirement is a worthy goal for all real estate investors, we all have to pay our bills along the way; equity (profit on paper) will not feed you and your family. A sound businessperson focuses first on generating cash flow, then on growing the business. The real estate business is no exception.

WHAT TO EXPECT FROM THIS BOOK

This book will teach you, step-by-step, how to generate cash by buying and quickly reselling (aka flipping) properties. In Chapter 1, you will be introduced to the basic concepts of flipping properties. Chapter 2 covers the necessary mechanics of real estate transactions. In Chapters 3, 4, and 5 you will learn how to locate, analyze, and negotiate the purchase of a bargain property. In the later chapters, you will learn how to renovate, finance, and sell your properties for a healthy cash profit. In addition, we will review the appropriate legal and tax issues and give you a game plan for launching a successful investment career. In the appendixes, you will find valuable legal forms, contracts, step-by-step checklists, and sample advertising and marketing materials.

Are you a beginner looking to generate some immediate cash? Perhaps you are working full-time and are trying to obtain additional income or find a new career. Possibly you are up to your ears in debt and see no way of paying off your credit cards. Regardless of your personal situation, this book will help you earn the cash you need to accomplish your goals.

CHAPTER 1

The Concept of Flipping Properties

Real estate, like any other commodity, is bought and sold every day of the week. Many people become real estate agents because they know a small piece of a large pie means big bucks. Agents help facilitate a sale by finding a willing buyer for a willing seller, earning a commission of 4 percent to 7 percent of the sales price for making the deal happen.

It is relatively simple to get a real estate license, and real estate sales is a lucrative field for many people. As you may expect, however, strong competition exists among agents, and those who are successful work long, hard hours. In fact, most agents are on call weekends and nights, with their cell phones glued to their ears. Furthermore, real estate agents are required to take continuing-education classes and follow strict guidelines set forth by bureaucratic agencies. There are better ways for an entrepreneur to make a living!

THE FLIPPER

Investors who flip houses accomplish the same basic task that real estate agents accomplish. Specifically, the flipper investor buys real estate with the intention of immediately reselling for profit. As a flipper, he buys properties at substantially less than the going or retail rate. He acts as both principal and middleman, buying at one price, then reselling at a higher price.

If a deal is marginal (with not much profit) and he adds no value to the property, the flipper's profit is commensurate to that of a real estate agent. Unlike an agent, however, the flipper may have only a few hours of his time tied up in the deal. Furthermore, the flipper's upside profit potential is much higher than an agent's commission, for an occasional bargain purchase can bring a tremendous return. The flipper does not need a license to practice, nor is he under the watchful eye of a government agency. He benefits from low overhead and flexible work hours and he doesn't have to drive a Mercedes to be taken seriously (although he can certainly afford one!).

THE DIFFERENT TYPES OF FLIPPERS

There are three types of flipper investors, which usually are based on experience:

- The scout
- The dealer
- The retailer

The Scout

The scout is an information gatherer. She finds potential deals and sells the information to other investors, much like a bird dog that brings ducks back to his master. Many people get started as a scout for other investors because it does not take any cash or prior knowledge to look for distressed properties.

What Is a Distressed Property?

A distressed property is one that creates emotional or financial distress for its owner. Distress may be caused by the owner's financial problems or the fact that the property is in need of repair. Either way, the owner is motivated to sell the property at a discounted price. ■

The scout finds a property for sale, gathers the necessary information, and then provides this information to investors for a fee. The fee varies, depending on the price of the property and the profit potential. The scout can expect to make $500 to $1,000 each time she provides information that leads to a purchase by another investor.

The scout should gather as much information about a property as she can find, such as:

- The complete address of the property
- The owner's name and telephone number
- A photograph of the house
- Information about the owner's asking price and loan balance, and whether the payments are current
- Liens on the property

- Summary of information about the condition of the property
- Information about the owner's motivation to sell (e.g., foreclosure, needs repairs, divorce, etc.)

Will Someone Steal the Deal?

The beginning scout may be wary of providing too much information to investors for fear of someone stealing the deal. This rarely happens, because experienced investors know that the unhappy scout will not bring any future deals their way. ▪

The scout may speak to the owner directly or gather information from public records or other means, as we will discuss in Chapter 3. The scout's most important job is to identify a property owner who is motivated to sell at a discounted price. Keep in mind that a house in need of repair does not necessarily indicate its owner is motivated to sell. Many property owners can afford to fix a property or let it sit vacant for months or even years. The motivated seller does not have the means or the will to handle the problems presented by the property.

For example, a scout drives by a boarded-up house with an overgrown lawn and old newspapers piled up on the stoop. The scout speaks with a neighbor and learns the name and telephone number of the owner. The scout then talks with the owner and discovers that the property is in foreclosure and that the owner does not have the means to repair the property or make up the mortgage payments. The owner is open to all suggestions, but the scout has neither the means nor the experience to solve the owner's problem. The scout sells the information she has gathered about the property and its owner to another investor.

The Dealer

The dealer, like the scout, locates deals for other investors. He finds a bargain property and signs a purchase contract with the owner. He then can close on the property and sell it outright, or just sell his contract to another investor (see Chapter 2). He is providing more than just information; he is controlling the property with a binding purchase contract. The dealer often puts up earnest money to secure the deal, so he assumes more risk than the scout does. Because the dealer controls the property with a purchase contract, he has greater profit potential than the scout does.

The dealer often resells the property in its "as is" condition. Dealers, however, can sometimes increase their profits by cleaning up their properties. In fact, a simple cleanup job may increase the dealer's profit by several thousand dollars. While most investors can see past the mess, a spruced-up property is psychologically more appealing to any buyer, even an experienced one. The dealer does not need to perform repairs or upgrades, but simply clean up the appearance of the property by removing junk and debris, cleaning windows, and cutting the lawn. This type of labor can be hired out for a few hundred dollars. Don't pay a premium price for a professional cleaning crew that advertises with a full-page ad in the Yellow Pages. Check the classified ads of your newspapers or the local *Pennysaver* for a mom-and-pop operation with a pickup truck, a broom, some trash bags, and an old lawn mower!

Dealers can flip as many deals as they can find. On a full-time basis, a dealer can make well over $15,000 a month without ever fixing a property or dealing with a tenant. On a part-time basis, a dealer could easily make an extra $3,000 a month flipping a property or two. The dealer's lifestyle is that of a true entrepreneur; he can work as much or as little as he likes, with no boss and no employees and the freedom to do as he pleases!

The Retailer

The retailer usually buys a property from a dealer or with the assistance of a real estate agent or scout. The retailer's goal is to fix up the property so she can sell it for full retail price to an owner-occupant. Compared to other flippers, the retailer puts up the most money, takes the most risk, and stands to make the largest profit on each deal. However, it may take the retailer months to realize her profit, unlike the scout or dealer who makes his money in a matter of days or weeks.

Before one can become a successful retailer, she must have working knowledge of how to renovate a house, particularly the cost of doing so. A good dealer should have a rough idea of the cost of repairs as well, so that he can buy properties at the right price and resell them to the retailer. A dealer who pays too much for a property will have a difficult time reselling it to the retailer. Likewise, the retailer who pays too much will have a difficult time making a profit upon resale to an owner-occupant.

The retailer is limited by her financial resources and the number of properties she can rehab at once. Each deal should be evaluated separately; it is sound business practice to act at times as a dealer and other times as a retailer.

FIND THE BACK DOOR FIRST

Every investor should have a means to sell properties quickly. You should never enter into a real estate transaction without knowing your exit strategy. Are you going to flip the property to another investor or are you going to fix it up and sell it retail? How much money or labor are you going to put into the property? How long do you expect to hold it? How long do you think it will take to sell? These are important questions you need to answer before you make an offer to purchase a property.

When you are getting started, you can sell your first few deals to investors to generate working capital. You should not be greedy, but you can expect to make $1,000 to $3,000 on your first flip. You do not have to own a property to make money from it. You simply need to control the property by putting it under contract. Once you have located a potential deal and secured it with a purchase contract, you can sell your deal to another investor for a profit.

Example: You find a property worth about $100,000 in its current state. It requires $10,000 to renovate the property. In its best condition, the property is worth $115,000. You negotiate a purchase price of $80,000 and sign a purchase contract with the owner. You find another investor who is willing to pay $82,000 for the property and do the necessary repairs. Thus, you can sell your deal to another investor for $2,000 and walk away with a nice profit using no money of your own. The other investor will make a nice profit as well.

In this example, the property was purchased at a 20 percent discount from its current market value. This discount may vary widely, depending on the property, the neighborhood, the condition of the real estate market, and how many repairs the property needs. A precise approach to making offers will be discussed later in this book.

Keep in mind that the retailer you sell the property to will make more money than you will on the deal. Do not let his profit potential bother you. There is enough room for both of you to profit, and, unlike the retailer, you assume little risk.

Join an Investment Club

A real estate investors club in your area is an excellent place to meet other dealers and retailers. A complete list of local groups can be found at <www.creonline.com/clubs.htm>. If there are no clubs in your area, consider forming one. You can find other local investors by reading the classified ads section of your newspaper under the Real Estate Wanted and Private Money to Loan sections. You can also run a classified ad under the Investment Properties section. In addition, ask some of the local real estate agents and the local landlords or apartment association for names of local investors.

Run a Classified Ad

If you have a property under contract and are looking for a retailer, run a classified ad in a local newspaper. Try a few different newspapers and ads (see Appendix B for a few sample ads). Log the calls you receive to track the effectiveness of the ad. More important, keep information about the people who call and the types of properties they like. Don't waste too much time with inexperienced investors, for they probably don't have the means to buy properties from you. Qualify the callers with the following questions:

- How many houses do you buy each year?
- What type of discount do you usually look for on properties?
- Do you have your own cash to close or will you borrow it?
- How big a renovation can you handle?
- If I find a bargain, how quickly can you close?

If you ask these questions, you will quickly have a list of investors to call when a new project comes along. If you don't have an investment club in your area, this is how you will meet other investors!

Selling Properties Retail

Many beginning investors try to sell a property without a real estate agent to save money on commissions. They also neglect to include the agent's commission in their estimate of costs for the property. If you are selling a property retail to an owner-occupant, failing to use an agent is a mistake. In fact, a majority of sellers who start out selling their properties without agents end up listing the properties with agents after being unsuccessful on their own.

Most real estate agents do not aggressively market properties; however, they place the information on the Multiple Listing Service (MLS), which is used by all other real estate agents. Because most properties are sold through the MLS and the largest pool of qualified buyers work through real estate agents, the odds of finding a qualified buyer quickly are greatest when the property is listed on the MLS. Furthermore, you can focus your efforts on finding more deals rather than waiting for buyers to show up at your property.

Contrary to what agents would like you to believe, most do little to market your particular property other than post a colorful sign and list the property on the MLS. Thus, find an agent you like to work with who is willing to give you a discount for repeat business and help you find other potential deals. A growing trend is for an agent to offer a listing at a flat fee, rather than at a percentage of the selling price. If you are doing business in a state in which the real estate agents draft the purchase contract, make sure your agent is competent and experienced and can guide you through the paperwork as a beginning investor.

Not every property can be resold quickly. Oftentimes, you may be stuck with a property for a few months. If you do your homework, this will rarely happen. If you cannot resell a property within 30 days, you probably made a mistake. Either you paid too much, underestimated repairs, or picked the wrong neighborhood.

GETTING RID OF DIFFICULT PROPERTIES

Sometimes you may sign up a marginal deal and have a difficult time reselling it. Even though you are looking for quick cash, there are other ways to make a profit. For example, you can take a promissory note (a written, legal promise to pay) from your investor-buyer for part or the entire purchase price. This note will be secured with a lien on the property (a mortgage or deed of trust, as discussed in Chapter 2) and will contain interest payments. Or you can tell the investor you will accept a promissory note for the purchase price, with no payments due until he resells the property.

Another Option: Partner with a Retailer

If a deal is rather thin and needs a lot of work, the retailer to whom you sell it may not have enough cash to pay you. In that case, become partners with the retailer. If you are flipping to an investor who will rehab the property, offer the property as your share of the partnership while he offers the materials and the work as his share. When you sell the property, you split the proceeds. You may have to take less than half of the net profit to make the deal work.

Minimize Your Loss

Sometimes you sign a purchase contract for a bad house. A bad house is one that you cannot sell for a reasonable profit. The problem may be a combination of paying too much, bad market timing, unforeseen repairs, or just plain bad luck. Keep in mind that you can always sell the house for what you paid or even take a loss if you have a lot of cash invested. Sometimes you have to move on and stop the financial bleeding. You must remember that when you make an offer, you have to include enough room in the deal for someone other than you to make a profit (see Chapter 4). Many beginners make this mistake. You cannot resell a property to another investor and make a profit if she cannot profit as well. If you expect to make too much profit and hold on to a property too long, you will lose out in the long run. When you are flipping properties as a dealer, the goal is moving them fast—don't get greedy!

Key Points to Remember

- A flipper buys property with the intent of quick resale.
- There are three types of flippers—the scout, the dealer, and the retailer.
- A flipper may act as a dealer on some transactions and a retailer on others.
- Establish a network of other investors to buy your properties.
- Use the MLS to sell your retail properties.
- Cut your losses on bad deals.

CHAPTER 2

The Mechanics of Real Estate Transactions

Whether you are a novice investor or an experienced one, you must have a working knowledge of the legal aspects of real estate transactions. You need to understand the paperwork involved in a real estate transaction, or you are at the mercy of those who do know. Furthermore, your risk of making an expensive mistake or missing an opportunity increases tremendously.

THE DEED

A deed is a written instrument used to convey ownership to property. You must know how to draft a deed because at times you may need to get one signed in a hurry. If you are dealing with a seller in foreclosure, a "kitchen table" deed is very common, so you need to know how to draft and execute one in such a situation. If another investor is offering you a deed that he received from someone in foreclosure across a kitchen table, you must make sure that deed was drafted and executed properly.

Types of Deeds

Deeds differ usually by the type of guarantee or warranty that they give. There are basically four different types of deeds:

General Warranty Deed: Also referred to as a warranty deed, this is the most complete guarantee of title. The warranty deed promises that the grantor (seller) has full and complete title and forever warrants against any claims against the title. If anyone makes a claim to the property, no matter how old the claim is, the grantor of a warranty deed must fix the problem. If you are receiving a deed, you must insist on getting a general warranty deed. There are exceptions to this rule, but a general warranty deed is the best deed. If a lending institution is financing the transaction, it will probably insist on a warranty deed.

Special Warranty Deed: This type of deed only warrants that the grantor has acquired title and did nothing to impair it while he held title. This is roughly the equivalent of a grant deed (which is used in California). Public officials, such as a sheriff, use a special warranty deed after a foreclosure sale.

Bargain and Sale Deed: This type of deed has no express warranties, but usually contains a statement of consideration paid and an implication that the grantor has some title or interest in the property.

Quitclaim Deed: A quitclaim deed contains no promises or warranties. The grantor simply gives up whatever claim he may or may not have. A quitclaim deed is commonly used to transfer an interest between spouses or to clear up a title defect. If the seller has good title, he can transfer the property with a quitclaim deed the same as he could with a warranty deed. However, the grantor makes no guarantee that title is good. You should consider using a quitclaim deed whenever you give title.

Elements of the Deed

A deed must contain certain elements to be considered a legal and valid transfer. Make sure when you execute a deed or pay someone else for a deed to real estate that the following elements are present:

Must Be in Writing: Generally speaking, any instrument affecting an interest in real estate must be in writing to be enforceable. It does not necessarily need to be typed, but it may not be accepted for public recording if it is not legible.

Parties to the Transaction: The deed must state the giver of the deed (grantor) and the receiver of the deed (grantee). The grantor's name must be spelled exactly as it appears on the deed that gave him title, even if that spelling is incorrect. In community property states (Arizona, California, Florida, Idaho, Louisiana, Nevada, New Mexico, Texas, and Washington), the law presumes that both spouses own all marital assets, regardless of how they are titled. Thus, you also need a separate quitclaim deed from the grantor's spouse, even if her name does not appear on title.

Consideration: The deed must state that the grantor received consideration even though no actual money changed hands. You can insert the purchase price or simply the words: "The grantee has paid ten dollars in hand and other good and valuable consideration, the sufficiency of which is hereby acknowledged."

Legal Description: The legal description of the property must appear exactly as it does in the previous deed. It will usually read something like "Lot 25, Block 21, Harris Subdivision, County of Barrington, State of Illinois." This designation comes from a plat map that was previously filed in the county records. If the description is more complicated than a simple lot and block or government survey description, simply photocopy the description from the previous deed and insert it into the new deal.

Words of Conveyance: This language spells out what type of deed is given. It usually reads something like "The grantor hereby grants, conveys, and warrants" (warranty deed) or "the grantor hereby remises, releases, and quitclaims" (quitclaim deed).

Signature of the Grantor: The grantor must sign her name exactly as her name appears. If the grantor is not available for signature, an authorized agent or attorney-in-fact can sign on her behalf. This process is accomplished by a power of attorney that authorizes an agent to act for the grantor to sign a deed. The power of attorney should include a legal description of the property and should be recorded in county records with the deed that is signed by the agent. The agent does not sign the grantor's name, but rather signs his own name as attorney-in-fact for the grantor.

Acknowledgment: The deed should be acknowledged before a notary public. An acknowledgment is a declaration that the person signing is who she claims she is and that she is signing voluntarily. The notary signs the deed, affirming that the grantor appeared before him and that he knows the person or was provided with sufficient proof of identity. Although acknowledgment is not required to make a deed valid, it is usually required for recording. The proper form of acknowledgment differs from state to state, so make certain your deed complies with your state's law.

Practical Tip: Have a Notary on Call

Oftentimes, you will buy a property with a seller signing a deed over a kitchen table. Because the signature of the seller must be notarized, you need to have a notary on call. Look in your local Yellow Pages under Notary Publics. Virtually every city has a notary with a pager who will show up on 30 minutes' notice!

Delivery

Title does not pass until a deed is delivered to the grantee. Thus, a deed signed but held in escrow does not convey title until the escrow agent delivers the deed. Many people are under the mistaken impression that title passes when a deed is recorded. While recording a deed is common practice, it is not required to convey title to real estate.

RECORDING DOCUMENTS

The recording system gives constructive notice to the public of the transfer of an interest in property. Recording simply involves bringing the original document to the local county courthouse or county clerk's office. The original document is copied onto a computer or microfiche and then is returned to the new owner. In addition, the county tax assessor usually requires filing a "real property transfer declaration," which contains some basic information about the sale. There is a filing fee for recording the deed, which runs $6 to $10 per page. In addition, the county, city, and/or state may assess a transfer tax based on either the value of the property or the selling price (often called documentary stamps).

A deed or other conveyance does not have to be recorded to be a valid transfer of an interest. For example, what happens if John gives a deed to Mary, then he gives it again to Fred and Fred records it first? What happens if John gives a mortgage to ABC Savings & Loan, but the mortgage is not filed for six months and then John borrows from another lender who records its mortgage first? Who wins and who loses in these scenarios?

Most states follow a "race-notice" rule, which means that the first person to record his document wins so long as:

- He received title in good faith.
- He paid value.
- He had no notice of a prior transfer.

Example: John buys a home and in doing so, he borrows $75,000 from ABC Savings & Loan. John signs a promissory note and a mortgage pledging his home as collateral. ABC messes up the paperwork and the mortgage does not get recorded for 18 months. In the interim, John borrows $12,000 from The Money Store, for which he gives a mortgage as collateral. The Money Store records its mortgage, unaware of John's unrecorded first mortgage to ABC. The Money Store will now have a first mortgage on the property.

NOTES AND MORTGAGES

Most people think of going to a bank to get a mortgage. Actually, we go to the bank to get a loan. Once we are approved for the loan, we sign a promissory note to the lender, which is our promise to pay. We also give (not get) a mortgage as security for repayment of the note. A mortgage (also called a deed of trust in some states) is a security agreement under which the borrower pledges his property as collateral for payment. The mortgage document is recorded in the property records, creating a lien on the property in favor of the lender.

If the underlying obligation (the promissory note) is paid off, the lender must release the collateral (the mortgage). A release is accomplished by signing a release of mortgage, which is recorded in the county property records. The release will remove the mortgage lien from the property. If you search the public records of a particular property, you will see many recorded mortgages that have been placed and released over the years.

Deed of Trust

About half the states use a document called a deed of trust rather than a mortgage. A complete list of foreclosure rules and types of security used can be found in Appendix D. The deed of trust is a document in which the trustor (borrower) gives a deed to a neutral third party (trustee) to hold for the beneficiary (lender). A deed of trust is worded almost exactly the same as a mortgage. Thus, the deed of trust and the mortgage are essentially the same, other than in the foreclosure process. Foreclosure is a legal proceeding by which a lender attempts to force the sale of a property to recoup the money loaned to the homeowner.

PRIORITY OF LIENS

Liens, like deeds, are "first in time, first in line." If a property is owned free and clear, a mortgage recorded will be a first mortgage. A mortgage recorded later in time will be a second mortgage (sometimes called a junior mortgage). Likewise, any judgments or other liens recorded later are also junior liens. Holding a first mortgage is a desirable position, because a foreclosure on a mortgage can wipe out all liens that are recorded after it (called junior lien holders). The process of foreclosure will be discussed in more detail in Chapter 3.

The Basic Loan Transaction

At the closing of a typical real estate sale, the seller conveys a deed to the buyer. Most buyers obtain loans from conventional lenders for most of the cash needed for the purchase price. As discussed earlier, the lender gives the buyer cash to pay the seller, and the buyer gives the lender a promissory note. The buyer also gives the lender a security instrument (mortgage or deed of trust) under which she pledges the property as collateral. When the transaction is complete, the buyer has the title recorded in her name and the lender has a lien recorded against the property.

The Typical Owner-Carry Transaction

Rather than receiving all cash for the purchase price, a seller may accept a promissory note for all or part of the price. If the seller owns the property free and clear (i.e., no mortgage) and accepts a promissory note for all or part of the purchase price, the buyer will execute a mortgage or deed of trust to the seller. When the transaction is complete, the buyer has title recorded in his name and the seller has a lien (mortgage or deed of trust) on the property.

In some cases, the seller may already have a mortgage on the property. If this is the case, the seller may require the buyer to pay most of the purchase price in the form of cash so that he can satisfy his loan balance. The difference between the loan balance and the purchase price (equity) is paid in the form of a promissory note. Assuming the buyer borrows the cash from a conventional lender, the note to the seller will be secured by a mortgage that is junior or subordinate to the lender's mortgage. When the transaction is complete and all documents are recorded, the buyer has title recorded in his name, the lender has a first lien, and the seller has a second lien on the property, as shown in Figure 2.1.

FIGURE 2.1
Typical Owner Carry

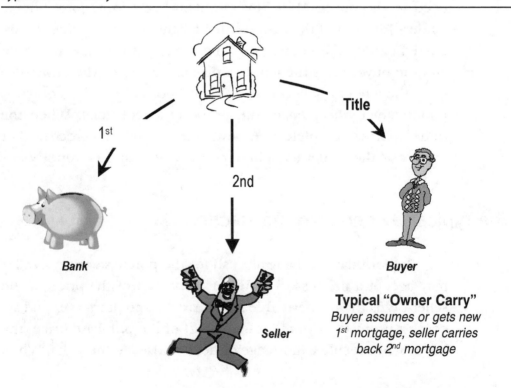

1st

2nd

Title

Bank

Seller

Buyer

Typical "Owner Carry"
Buyer assumes or gets new
1st mortgage, seller carries
back 2nd mortgage

ASSUMABLE VERSUS NONASSUMABLE MORTGAGES

Some properties have freely assumable mortgages, that is, the buyer does not have to qualify with a lender to take over the seller's loan. Buying a property with an assumable mortgage is desirable for two reasons. First, the buyer does not need good credit to qualify for the loan. Second, the buyer does not have to pay the costs (several thousand dollars) associated with obtaining a new loan. Because the buyer in our case will be an investor, it is almost a crime for him to pay these loan costs when he is going to resell the property within a few months and pay off the balance of the loan.

The Due-on-Sale Clause

Many years ago, all loans were freely assumable, meaning anyone could purchase property by taking title and making payments on the existing loan. When interest rates began rising, lenders were competing with existing low-interest loans. Some banker figured out that this competition could be eliminated by placing restrictions on the transfer of property encumbered by a mortgage. Thus the due-on-sale clause was created.

The due-on-sale clause contained in a mortgage or deed of trust gives the lender the option to require complete payoff (aka acceleration) of the underlying loan if the property is sold or if the title is transferred. Most loans insured by the Federal Housing Authority (FHA) originated before December 15, 1989, and loans guaranteed by the Veterans Administration (VA) originated before March 1, 1988, are freely assumable, that is, these mortgages have no due-on-sale clauses. However, virtually all loans today contain due-on-sale clauses. If you take title to a property without paying off the loan, the bank has the right to call the loan due.

Taking title subject to property without paying off the mortgage loan or assuming liability for the debt is known as *taking subject to.* If the loan is freely assumable or if the lender approves of the transaction, you are *assuming* the loan; that is, you are agreeing to be personally liable for the debt. If you assume the loan, both you and the former owner are liable.

Contrary to popular belief, it is not a criminal act to transfer property with a mortgage containing a due-on-sale clause. A mortgage is simply a contract between the lender and the borrower, the breach of which gives the lender the right to call the loan due. If the lender does call the loan due and it is not paid off, the lender has the option of foreclosing the property.

Banks rarely enforce the due-on-sale clause anymore because the process of calling in loans is not profitable. When interest rates were high, it made financial sense for a bank to call in a 6 percent loan, forcing the borrower to refinance. However, the market interest rates are still relatively low, so it would not be profitable for a lender to call a loan due, especially if the payments are current. If market interest rates remain equal to or less than the rate of the loan you are concerned about being called due, chances are you will have no objection from the lender.

> Many people who own real property subject to a trust deed simply go ahead and transfer it, figuring the lender (who, after all, may be a large corporation at the other end of the country) won't find out. They are often right.
>
> Mary Randolph, *The Deeds Book—How to Transfer Title to California Real Estate,* 3rd ed. Nolo Press, 1994.

Third-party servicing companies handle the payments on most loans today. Thus, there is little chance that anyone is paying attention to the name on the checks that are received for the monthly payments. Even if you get caught, chances are you will sell the property before the lender can call the loan due.

THE DOUBLE CLOSING

As we will discuss in Chapter 8, a closing is a ceremonial process during which title is delivered by deed from the seller to the buyer. In some cases, you will buy and sell the property to a retailer in a back-to-back double closing (also called double escrow in some states). You do not need any of your own cash to purchase the property from the owner before reselling it to the retailer in a double closing.

Here's how it works:

- *STEP 1.* The dealer signs a written agreement to purchase a property from the owner.
- *STEP 2.* The dealer signs a written contract with the retailer under which the retailer agrees to buy the property from the dealer at a higher price.
- *STEP 3.* The only party coming to the table with cash is the retailer. Assuming the retailer is borrowing money from a lender to fund the transaction, the retailer's bank will wire the funds into the bank account of the attorney, escrow agent, or title company (called the closing agent) who performs the closing.
- *STEP 4.* The owner signs a deed to the dealer, which is not delivered but deposited in escrow with the closing agent.
- *STEP 5.* The dealer signs a deed to the retailer that is deposited in escrow with the closing agent.
- *STEP 6.* The retailer signs the bank loan documents, at which point the transaction is complete.
- *STEP 7.* The closing agent delivers the funds to the owner for the purchase price, the difference to the dealer.
- *STEP 8.* The closing agent records the two deeds, one after another, at the county land records office.

As you can see, the dealer brought no cash to the table. His funds came from the proceeds of the second sale. If the second sale does not happen, the first transaction, which is closed in escrow, is not complete. The deal is dead.

Lender Seasoning Requirements

In recent years, some lenders have been placing title seasoning requirements on loan transactions. These lenders are afraid to fund the second part of a double closing because they fear the retailer's purchase price is inflated. As a result, they have placed seasoning requirements on the seller's ownership. If the seller (in this case, the dealer) has not owned the property for at least 12 months, the lender will assume that the deal is fishy and refuse to fund the retailer's loan. There really is no solution to this issue other than to deal with other lenders who don't have the seasoning hangup. If you are a real estate dealer, make sure you ask your retailer (or whomever you sell the property to) whether his lender has seasoning requirements. Another way around the seasoning issue is to assign your contract to the buyer, in which case the seller would be the current owner.

Flipping Is Not Illegal

There has been a lot of negative press lately about flipping and double closings. Scores of people have been indicted under what the press has called "property-flipping schemes." This misdescribed activity has nothing to do with the type of practices taught in this book. Uninformed lenders, real estate agents, and title companies will tell you that flipping is illegal. In fact, flipping is nothing of the sort.

The so-called property-flipping schemes work as follows: Unscrupulous investors sell properties to each other multiple times at progressively higher prices to artificially enhance the value of the property. They often do substandard repairs to the property. The final sale is to an unsophisticated buyer at an inflated price. In most cases, the seller, appraiser, and mortgage broker conspire by submitting fraudulent loan documents and bogus appraisals. The end result is a buyer who paid too much for a house and cannot afford the loan. Because many of these loans are insured by the Federal Housing Authority (FHA), the Senate has held hearings to investigate this practice.

Despite the negative press, flipping itself is not illegal. The activities described previously simply amount to loan fraud, nothing more: "While flipping itself is not illegal, it crosses the line when sellers falsify documents to lure buyers and lenders, including the Federal Housing Authority, into investing more money in a house than it is worth."
—Permanent Subcommittee on Investigations ▪

ASSIGNMENT OF CONTRACT

Another way to accomplish the same task as a double closing is to assign your purchase contract. Assigning a contract is similar to double-endorsing a check. You assign your rights under the contract to another investor for a fee. The investor closes directly with the owner in your place, like a pinch hitter. This also is a solution to the lender seasoning issue. If the buyer closes directly with the owner, the seasoning issue is solved.

Advantages of Using an Assignment

There are several advantages of using the contract assignment over a double closing. First, your name does not appear on the title for the world to see. Your business affairs can be kept private, as they should be. Furthermore, the sale at a lower price does not appear on the MLS, which can skew the appraisal when the retailer resells the property (see the discussion on appraisals in Chapter 4). Also, you save closing costs by not having a regular closing. Finally, you get your money fast, whether or not the other investor closes on the property.

Disadvantages of Using an Assignment

The main disadvantage of the contract assignment is that it is harder to sell. A closing usually is conducted at a title company or attorney's office while a contract assignment may not be. Unless the investor knows you personally, he may be wary of buying your contract. The contract assignment requires the investor to do his own due diligence regarding the title to the property, the legality of the contract, and whether or not the seller will live up to it when it comes time to close. Thus, you may not get as much money for a contract assignment as you would if you did a double closing and gave the investor a bona fide deed.

The second disadvantage of the contract assignment is that the investor knows what you are paying for the property. An unscrupulous investor may try to go around you and deal directly with the property owner. The solution to this challenge is to record a memorandum of agreement in county land records (see the sample form in Appendix C). This form is simply an affidavit signed by you that states you have a contract with the seller. Once recorded, this affidavit becomes a cloud on the seller's title. A cloud is an uncertainty regarding ownership. This uncertainty makes it difficult to insure title (as we will discover in the next chapter, title insurance may be a necessary part of a real estate transaction).

If the seller and the unscrupulous investor try to close the deal, the title company would discover the cloud on the seller's title and would probably refuse to insure the transaction. The cloud on title will effectively prevent the seller from selling the property to anyone but you, the party he originally agreed to sell it to. In this situation, the seller or the unscrupulous investor would have to pay you ransom to step out of the deal (which, by the way, is done by you signing a quitclaim deed).

Key Points to Remember

- Understand the basic mechanics of real estate transactions.
- Use double closings and contract assignments to flip properties.

CHAPTER 3

Proven Ways
to Find the Deals

In Chapter 1, we discussed the importance of buying distressed properties, which in reality means finding distressed owners. Finding these owners is an art that takes years to master. Finding motivated sellers requires advertising, marketing, salesmanship, and, like any business, keeping your nose to the ground.

The most common problem new investors face is finding bargain properties. Many who start out in real estate investing quit without ever buying their first property. They go through the motions of looking for deals for a few weeks or months and then decide it doesn't work. They forget that finding motivated sellers is similar to the salesperson finding his first customer—it takes persistence and hard work.

You cannot put together a deal without a motivated seller and you can only convince a motivated seller to accept unusual terms or sell at a discounted price. A motivated seller has a very good and pressing reason to sell the property below market. Before you start looking for motivated sellers, you must first realize that the vast majority of property owners are not motivated to sell.

FIND THE MOTIVATED SELLER

At the cost of sounding redundant, the concept is simple: Find motivated sellers who are willing to sell their properties at a discounted price. The appropriate discount will be discussed in the next chapter. Currently, the real estate market in most parts of the country is hot, hot, hot! Many people are complaining that the strength of the market precludes investors from finding deals on properties. The popular misconception is that in a rising market, even the most motivated seller can find a buyer for her property at full market price.

The truth is, you can work the concept of flipping properties in any market. Real estate legend A.D. Kessler once said, "There are no problem properties, just problem ownerships." The definition of a motivated seller fits squarely within Kessler's idea. A logical person knows that time, money, and effort can solve virtually any real estate problem. However, some people are too emotional about their real estate problems or have other motivating issues to deal with. Some of these issues include:

- Divorce
- Lack of concern
- Inexperience with real estate repairs
- Time constraints
- Death of a loved one
- Job transfer
- Landlording headaches
- Impending foreclosure and other financial problems

In conclusion, if you deal only with motivated sellers, you will be able to negotiate the right price and terms.

USE THE NEWSPAPER

An obvious, yet often overlooked, place to look for deals is in your local newspaper in the Real Estate Classified section. Be prepared to make a lot of calls, because finding properties is a numbers game. Do not waste much time with each seller; just ask basic questions to gather information about the property and the seller's needs. We will discuss the right questions to ask in Chapter 5, "The Art of Negotiating the Deal."

Most people you call cold out of the paper will not be responsive to you. Don't take it personally, just keep calling. Remember that each time you hear a "no," you will be one call closer to a "yes," and you will be learning along the way. If you live in a large metropolitan area, start with the ads for the areas you know. If you live in a more remote area, call every ad in the newspaper.

Private Owner Ads

Call on the ads that are for sale by owner (they don't all say for sale by owner, but you will learn which ones are). You will notice that real estate agents place many of the ads. You do not need to call on most of those ads, for there is a better way to deal with real estate agents (as discussed in the following section).

If you are not inspired to call on every ad, then at a minimum, call on the ads with key phrases. Examples of these key phrases are *must sell, fix-up, needs work, handyman special, vacant, motivated,* and so on. Unusually long ads listing every detail about the property are probably from inexperienced or motivated sellers, so these ads also warrant a call.

Real Estate Agent Ads

Believe it or not, many of the ads placed by real estate agents are teaser ads designed to get you calling about a particular type of house or neighborhood in which the agent works. Agents often pull the old bait and switch once you call and will do anything to get you into their office so they can show you other properties.

If the ad is for a property in one of your target neighborhoods, then call the agent for a different reason: to let him know what kind of properties you like. Call on all of the ads that advertise fixer properties in your target areas and ask for the agent's fax number. Fax him a brief letter, alerting him that you are an investor, that you are looking for fixer properties, and that you can close quickly if the price is right. A sample fax can be found in Appendix B. You should fax this letter to no less than 25 real estate offices in your first month of doing business. This letter will get the agents calling you for properties, rather than the other way around.

Properties for Rent

Another way to find deals is by calling the newspaper ads offering houses for rent. Most cities have more properties for rent than for sale. One reason is that some people become accidental landlords for one reason or another. For example, they may have inherited the property from their parents, or the owner may be a recently widowed woman whose husband previously handled the properties. These people are renting out the properties because they don't know what else to do with them.

Calling rental ads can be lucrative because some landlords are simply tired of tenant and property management issues. These landlords may want a way out of handling their problem property. You just don't know what the landlord's needs are until you ask, so consider calling on these ads for rent. Just pick up the phone and say, "I saw your ad in the paper for a property you are renting. I am also an investor. Are you interested in selling the property?" If the answer is "no," give him your name and telephone number and ask that he call you when he decides to sell. Also, ask him if he knows any other landlords in the area that may be interested in selling.

Making a lot of telephone calls does not excite most people, but the telephone can make you a lot of money. Telephone negotiating will be discussed further in Chapter 5.

Run Your Own Newspaper Ad

Run your own newspaper ad in the Real Estate Classified section to encourage motivated owners to call you. Many distressed sellers won't take the time or make the effort to advertise their property, so you need to flush them out. Run a simple three-line ad, such as:

We Buy Houses for Cash
Any Condition, Fast Closing
(555) 555-5555

Run this ad under the Real Estate Wanted section in the major newspapers and small local all-advertisement papers, such as *Pennysaver* and *Thrifty Nickel.* You can also run it under Money to Loan to attract property owners in foreclosure. We have provided you with other sample ads in Appendix B.

Classified ads should be run every day of the week, not just on Sundays. Call your newspaper and ask for the bulk or long-term rate. This rate may require you to commit to six months or more of advertising. You should consider running the ad for at least six months to determine whether it is worthwhile. Do not be discouraged if you see seven other ads just like yours. McDonald's and Burger King do more business when they are next door to each other. Likewise, your ad will pull just as many calls next to similar ads. Sometimes a motivated seller will choose to do business with you over someone else because of the sound of your voice or the fact that you like the Yankees. You just never know what motivates people, so place your ad in the newspaper and keep it there!

Call the Other Ads Yourself

As discussed in Chapter 1, a dealer needs to find a pool of retail investors to which he sells his properties. The other We Buy Houses ads are a great place to find these people. ■

Handling the Incoming Calls

Unless you have a business office, set up a separate telephone line in your home to handle incoming calls. If you are not available during the day to answer calls, have them forwarded to your cell phone (don't even consider not having a cell phone!). If you are working full-time at another profession, use a voice mail that screens out potentially motivated sellers.

Example: "Thank you for calling Real Estate Solutions, Inc. If you are calling about a house for sale, please leave your name, telephone number, the property address, and why you are selling."

This message will screen out the truly motivated sellers from the marginally motivated sellers who are simply looking to shop their properties.

REAL ESTATE AGENTS

Real estate agents can be either a great source of potential deals or a big stumbling block, depending on how you deal with them. They are among the most informed people regarding properties for sale, and they have access to more information than investors do. Agents also have many contacts and may know of potential deals that are not advertised on the MLS (called "pocket" listings).

Agent versus Broker

In most states, a person must be licensed as a broker to list property. A listing is an agreement between the seller and the broker that permits the broker to sell the property for a fee. In most cases, this fee is 6 percent or 7 percent of the sales price. The broker who signs this agreement with the seller is called the listing broker.

The listing broker usually hires several agents (sometimes called salespersons) to help sell the properties that he has listed. An agent, like a broker, must be licensed to sell real estate. In most states, however, only a broker can list a property. Thus, if the agent finds a buyer for the property, the listing broker and his agent split the commission for the sale. While a broker and an agent are different, we will refer to them synonymously as agent.

What Is a REALTOR®?

A REALTOR® is a registered trademark term reserved only for members of the local board of REALTORS®, which is affiliated with the National Association of REALTORS®. The boards are private, self-regulating agencies that govern rules of conduct for their members. Most agents belong to one or more local boards; membership is usually a requirement to obtain access to the MLS computer system. ■

The Buyer's Agent

A buyer's agent represents a buyer looking for properties. Most listed properties are placed on the MLS. The MLS is a computer database that allows agents to run computerized searches for properties meeting their buyers' criteria. Most listing agents will offer a co-op fee to any buyer's agent who procures a buyer to purchase the property. This co-op is a part of the listing agent's commission.

Example: A property is listed at $100,000 on the MLS. The listing agent's commission is 7 percent and he is offering a 3 percent co-op fee. The listing agent's fee would be $7,000 if he found a buyer for the property. If a buyer's agent found the buyer and the property was sold for $100,000 then the listing agent would get $4,000 and the buyer's agent would get $3,000.

The buyer's agent's loyalty and representation are to the buyer, although the buyer's agent is paid by sharing his commission with the listing agent. Because the buyer's agent usually procures the buyer to make the sale, he is often referred to as the selling agent.

Using a good buyer's agent will help you find a lot of deals. The agent can check the MLS for new properties for sale on a weekly basis. Also, ask her to search through the MLS for the motivation buzzwords, such as *must sell, needs work, estate sale, foreclosure, divorce, rehab,* etc. These buzzwords will locate distressed properties. Remember, distressed properties are those that create emotional or financial distress for their owners.

Make offers only on the distressed properties that are already priced below market. You may find it hard to believe, but many agents list properties in need of work at full market price! In addition, ask your agent to search the MLS in your target areas by price per square foot, which can also generate leads for bargains.

Although a buyer's agent can be an excellent source of leads, you should not use the agent as your primary source of leads when you get started. An agent is a businessperson and his time is valuable, so he may not be willing to spend much time with new investors. A busy agent does not want to waste his time with a beginning investor making frivolous offers that don't get accepted. In a strong market, there are plenty of qualified conventional homebuyers that an agent can work with. He doesn't need to deal with creative offers and nothing down, pie-in-the-sky promises. This view does not represent reality, yet it is how most agents think. As a beginner, you will get discouraged dealing with a buyer's agent who possesses this attitude, so make sure you approach him in the right way:

- Dress nicely. You want to look "money."
- Be respectful of his time—ask him to have his assistant fax you the listings you are looking for.
- Drive by the properties you are interested in before asking him to show you the inside of each property.
- Don't come off as a hotshot, but do let him know you intend to buy more than one property and that he will have repeat business. If you intend to sell the property retail,

offer him the listing (and, of course, ask for a discount on his fee for this listing).

MORTGAGE BROKERS

Mortgage companies spend thousands of dollars every week for advertisements and telemarketers to generate leads. They often receive hundreds of dead leads from people in distress with no equity and no ability to qualify for a new loan. Contact some local brokers and offer to pay them for these names. Many of these borrowers are behind in their loan payments and may be facing foreclosure. This information is invaluable because it is not made public until the lender commences foreclosure.

These borrowers may have little choice but to deal with you. Do not take advantage of them, because it will only hurt you in the end. Be fair, but only make a deal that is profitable for you.

BANK-OWNED PROPERTIES

Properties that are foreclosed by a bank are called REOs (short for real estate owned). Contact your local banks and ask for the REO department. Let them know you buy properties. Some may have special financing available for these properties. A list of Internet resources for bank REOs can be found in Appendix E.

FARMING NEIGHBORHOODS

Successful real estate agents utilize a technique called farming to increase their business activity. They pick a neighborhood or two and focus their marketing efforts within that area. You should try the same technique. Start with a neighborhood that is relatively convenient for you.

Drive the Area

Spend a few weekends driving around the area. The goal for you at first is to learn about the area, the style of houses, and the average prices. Over time, you may expand your farm area, but stay within areas that contain the type of homes you plan to purchase. It is not necessary to begin your investment career by learning every square mile of a large metropolitan area; it is important to learn the value of typical homes in your target areas. This knowledge will enable you to make quick decisions about whether a particular prospect is a bargain.

Attend Open Houses

Visit open houses and for sale by owner (FSBO) properties on weekends. Speak directly with the owners and their agents. Pass out your business cards. Make friends. Word of mouth and referrals are a big part of any business (see the discussion later in this chapter). Take a good look at the property and its physical features. After going to a couple dozen open houses in the neighborhood, you will get to know the value of the properties and the different styles of houses.

Look for Ugly and Vacant Properties

While you are driving around neighborhoods, look for vacant, ugly houses. How can you tell if a house is vacant? Look in the window! Of course, you should use a fair amount of discretion; this practice may get you shot, bitten by a dog, or arrested. First look for the obvious signs of vacancy—overgrown grass, no window shades, boarded windows, newspapers, garbage, mail piled up, etc. If you are not certain whether the property is vacant, knock on the door. If the owner answers, be polite and respectful and ask if he is interested in selling. In many cases, it may be a rental property, so ask the occupants for the name and telephone number of the owner. Obviously, you should not visit these properties alone, especially at night.

If the property is vacant, ask the neighbors if they know the owner. Most neighbors are helpful, for they know ugly houses hurt their own property values. In addition, ask the mailman—he knows all of the empty houses on the block. Leave a business card and write down the address of the ugly or vacant properties. When you get home, look up the name and address of the owner. Finding the owner of a vacant house can be difficult, which is why the persistent people who find the information make the most money. To determine the name of the owner, call your local tax assessor's office or look up the deed recorded with the county land records.

To contact the owner takes a little more digging. Try speaking with the neighbors or asking the post office for a copy of a change-of-address form on file for the property. Online services, such as at <www.infousa.com>, will search public databases, such as the Driver's License Bureau and the Department of Motor Vehicles for a small fee.

Some cities, towns, and counties will tag a house with code violations. This is often a sign of a neglected or vacant property. Ask your city if you can obtain a list of such properties or find where this information is publicly recorded.

Direct Mailing

Direct-mail marketers are masters at working the numbers game. They mail postcards, fliers, brochures, and catalogs by the tens of thousands to prospective customers. Believe it or not, direct-mail success is about 1 percent. That means a 99 percent failure rate! Here's a little secret: You can get filthy rich on a 1 percent success rate in direct mail.

Consider that a typical subdivision may have more than a thousand homes. If you were able to make $35,000 flipping 1 percent (ten homes) in that subdivision each year, you could operate a nice little side business. Expand your efforts into five areas, and you have a very nice living!

Postcards are the cheapest and most effective way to cover a neighborhood. Go to the post office and buy a couple thousand postcards. Take them to a printer and have a simple message printed on the postcard, such as "We Buy Houses" (see sample ads in Appendix B). Don't expect to get all of the calls at once; sometimes people call months after receiving your cards. Try mailing to the same people two or three times a year. You may get as many calls the second or third time around.

Promote Yourself

In addition to postcards, blanket the neighborhoods you choose with other marketing materials such as fliers and door hangers. When funds become available, consider more aggressive advertising, such as bus stop benches and supermarket shopping carts. When someone in the area is thinking of selling, she may call you before listing her property with an agent. By saving these people a real estate commission, you may be halfway to your desired purchase discount.

Distributing Fliers and Door Hangers: Don't spend your time passing out fliers and door hangers; rather, hire some kids to do it for you. Go back and check to see if the job is done before you pay them! Instruct them not to place anything inside a mailbox. The fliers should be stuck inside a screen door or fence. Door hangers are a bit more expensive than fliers, but they are easier to distribute, because you can hang them. Carry door hangers and fliers in your car when you cruise neighborhoods. Whenever you see a person in the yard or a for sale by owner sign, stop and talk with the owner, then hand him a flier.

Signs: Well-placed signs (aka bandit signs) can also attract sellers. Local sign-making franchise stores such as Next Day Signs can produce signs rather cheaply. If you don't have a store like this in your area, try <www.iprint.com>. Post these signs on street corners in target neighborhoods. *Warning:* Check with local authorities regarding laws for posting such signs; otherwise, you may receive a call asking you to remove them or to show up for a court date!

Magnetic car signs can also attract motivated sellers.

Share the Expense: Other unrelated businesses may be marketing their products or services in the same neighborhood using the same advertising means. Offer to split the expense to share your message. For example, if a pizzeria is distributing single-sided fliers, offer to pay for the printing if your message can appear on the back of the flier. Also, check with local companies that send coupon mailers in bulk. It is much cheaper to mail information when multiple advertisers are involved.

TARGETED DIRECT MAIL

Earlier, we talked about directing a blind mailing to a targeted area. Rather than a blind mailing, try mailing to specific lists, such as:

- Out-of-state owners (could also be motivated landlords or job transferees)
- People who have poor credit and own homes
- People with federal tax liens
- People in foreclosure or bankruptcy within the past year (they may have been bailed out, but are still in financial distress)

The names of these people can be purchased from a mailing-list broker. Look in your local Yellow Pages under Mailing List Companies. You should expect to pay 10¢ to 30¢ per name. In addition, keep a running list of the vacant houses, people who call on your ads, and other leads. Mail postcards to these people on a regular basis.

Color and Style of the Message: Many studies have been conducted by marketing companies to determine the most effective color, size, and content of the wording of marketing pieces. In other words, what makes people tick? While this information is somewhat useful, don't get caught up—the most important part of marketing is repetition. Keep sending the mail until the recipients ask to be taken off your list or a postcard comes back marked "deceased," then find out who the heirs of the estate are (see the following section).

PROBATE ESTATES

Every year, countless people die owning real estate in your city. Oftentimes, the property is in a state of disrepair because the owner neglected it during his final years or becomes so because it sat vacant after his death. When someone dies with real estate in his name, the ownership does not automatically vest in the heirs of the deceased's estate. The deceased's will must be processed through a court proceeding known as probate. The probate proceeding can take as much as a year or more in some areas, depending on the backlog of court cases, the amount of the deceased's assets, and the battling between the heirs for their share of the estate. The typical heirs to an estate are no different than the average person; they have no experience in fixing or selling real estate. If the heirs have no emotional attachment to the property, they will be eager for the administrator of the estate to liquidate the property quickly so that they can receive their inheritance in cash.

The easiest place to find probate properties is in the newspaper. The obituaries listings can be cross-referenced with real estate records in your county. If your county tax assessor has free online listings of properties, run the names of the deceased through the database to find a match. Once you have a match, contact the local probate court to find out the name of the administrator of the estate. Even though the particular situation may not present a deal for you, the administrator can keep your name on file in case she is the administrator of other estates.

GETTING REFERRALS

As an individual you can cover only a limited amount of ground looking for bargain properties. Because your greatest profit is made at the purchase end of a transaction, it makes sense to enlist others to help you find deals. In fact, you will find that after a few years in the real estate business, your greatest source of deals will be from referrals.

Get a Great Business Card

Get a nice business card. No, get a really nice business card. Don't be cheap and use the basic white ones from Office Depot, and don't even think about making one on your computer. When you are dealing with a $100,000 asset, look professional. Don't be shy about spending $200 or more on your business cards.

Your card should be double-sided, with a complete message about what it is you do (see Appendix B for some sample business cards). Your business should have a catchy name that tells what you do. CTM Investments tells people nothing; Real Estate Solutions, Inc. tells a lot more. You should form a corporation for your business as soon as possible (see Chapter 10).

Start with People You Know

Pass out your business cards to everyone you know, including business contacts. Let them know you are interested, hand them your card, then ask, "Can you think of anyone you know who may have a run-down property?" The best salespeople always use this technique—you should, too.

Other People in Your Farm Neighborhoods

Look for other people who are out working in your target neighborhoods each day. Mailmen, delivery people, contractors, insurance agents, city building and zoning inspectors, carpenters, and painters all make excellent scouts. Introduce yourself to these people and explain that you are looking for run-down, deserted, and ugly properties.

Enlist Scouts

You may start out in this business as a scout, but you will soon be a dealer or a retailer in need of a scout or two. You can offer people a referral fee for information leading to a property you purchase. This amount can be anything from $200 to $1,000, depending on how good the deal is. A friend who just stumbled across information about properties will be happy to comply. If you are looking for a real scout, however, it will be difficult to keep him motivated if he only gets paid when you buy a property.

Unfortunately, most beginners at any sales job quit after a few weeks because they lack the mental discipline to stick it out until their first commission check comes. A scout is no different, so you need to set up a modified payment structure to keep him interested. For example, you can pay him $20 for each ugly, vacant house he finds. The information should include a photograph of the house, the complete address, the owner's name, and information about the owner's distress (such as foreclosure, bankruptcy, divorce, etc.). You can also give him a couple hundred dollars as a bonus after you purchase the property.

FORECLOSURES

Chasing foreclosures is slang for following properties through the foreclosure process while attempting to entice the owners to sell. Foreclosure properties can be the best or the most frustrating source of leads. This is because the information is public and every seminar junkie in town is competing with you. To work the foreclosure market successfully, you must understand how the foreclosure process works.

Foreclosure is the legal process of the mortgage holder taking the collateral for a promissory note in default. The process is slightly different from state to state, but there are basically two types of foreclosure, judicial and nonjudicial. In mortgage states, judicial foreclosure is commonly used, while in deed-of-trust states, nonjudicial foreclosure is commonly used. Most states permit both types of proceedings, but it is common practice in most states to exclusively use one method or the other. A complete summary of each state's foreclosure rules can be found in Appendix D.

Judicial Foreclosure

Judicial foreclosure is a lawsuit that the lender (mortgagee) brings against the borrower (mortgagor) to get the property. About half of the states use judicial foreclosure. Like all lawsuits, foreclosure starts with a summons and a complaint served upon the borrower and any other parties with inferior rights in the property (remember, all junior liens, including tenancies, are wiped out by the foreclosure).

If the borrower does not file an answer to the lawsuit, the lender gets a judgment by default. A referee is then appointed by the court to compute the total amount (including interest and attorney's fees) that is due. The lender then must advertise a notice of sale in the newspaper for four to six weeks. If the total amount due is not paid, the referee conducts a public sale on the courthouse steps. The entire process can take as little as 3 months and as many as 12 months depending on the volume of court cases in that county.

The sale is conducted like an auction, because the property goes to the highest bidder. Unless there is significant equity in the property, the only bidder at the sale will be a representative of the lender. The lender can bid up to the amount it is owed, without having to actually come out of pocket with cash to purchase the property.

If the proceeds from the sale are insufficient to satisfy the amount owed to the lender, the lender may be entitled to a deficiency judgment against the borrower and anyone else who guaranteed the loan. Some states (e.g., California) prohibit a lender from obtaining a deficiency judgment against a borrower.

Nonjudicial Foreclosure

Many states permit a lender to foreclose without a lawsuit, using what is commonly called a power of sale. Rather than a mortgage, the borrower (grantor) gives a deed of trust to a trustee to hold for the lender (beneficiary). Upon default, the lender simply files a notice of default and a notice of sale, which is published in the newspaper. The entire process generally takes about 90 days. The borrower usually has a right of redemption after the sale (see the section on redemption that follows). In some states, mortgages also contain a power of sale.

Strict Foreclosure

A few states permit strict foreclosure, which does not require a sale. When the proceeding is started, the borrower has a certain amount of time to pay what is owed. Once that date has passed, title reverts to the lender.

Reinstating the Loan

Many states permit a borrower to cure the loan before the date of sale. This process simply requires paying the amount in arrears, plus interest and attorney's fees. It is certainly more desirable for a defaulting borrower to reinstate a loan rather than pay off the entire principal balance. Most deed-of-trust states permit the borrower to reinstate the loan before the sale.

Redemption Rights

Some states give a borrower the right to redeem the amount owed and get title to the property back after the sale. The length of the redemption period varies from state to state. Obtaining a deed from the owner during the redemption period gives you the right to redeem the property.

How to Get Foreclosure Deals

Deed from the Owner: The easiest way to deal with a foreclosure is to get the owner to deed you the property. Once you have the deed to the property, you are the owner. You can now try to negotiate a discount on the amount owed to the foreclosing lender. Many lenders will not deal with you unless you have written permission from the owner because releasing such information may violate Fair Credit Reporting Laws. It is a good idea to get a written authorization or a power of attorney from the seller along with the deed (see the sample form in Appendix C).

Attention: California Investors

If you buy a property from someone in foreclosure and it is their principal residence, you need to comply with Cal. Civ. Code Sec. 1695, which requires a five-day right of rescission and certain statutory language. ▪

The best way to get in touch with the owner is to knock on his door. This is not only gutsy, it is risky. You may be dealing with a bitter, belligerent person. More than likely you will be dealing with someone who is not being honest with himself about the situation. Don't try to bully the seller into giving you the deed. Just let him know that you are available, give him your business card, and check back from time to time. The more you follow up, the greater the chance that you will make a deal. At some point, the seller in foreclosure faces reality, and he will usually sell to the first person who comes banging on his door. The more you stay in touch, the greater the chance that you will be that person.

Getting Paid *Not* to Buy

Because many people in foreclosure are deluded into thinking they have options other than selling to you, offer the buy-out provision. In essence, your written contract will give the seller the right to cancel if she obtains a written offer better than yours before your closing date. That buyout fee is negotiable, but make sure it is enough to make it worth your while. ▪

Visit your local courthouse to find names of property owners in foreclosure. Better yet, subscribe to one of the local foreclosure listing services. These companies gather this information each week and sell it for a reasonable fee, saving you a great deal of time. The information you want to buy is the list of people in foreclosure, not properties that have been already foreclosed and have been taken back by the bank. Check your local Yellow Pages and ask other investors in your area which services are reputable. Some local companies are listed in Appendix C.

Buy the Property at the Sale: In a foreclosure, there is a public sale of the property in all but strict foreclosure states. Contact your local courthouse and ask where this sale will happen. Visit a few sales to watch the action before engaging in a bid. Don't be surprised if no one bids but the foreclosing lender. Most properties in foreclosure don't have enough equity to justify a bid from an investor.

To buy at the foreclosure sale, you must bring certified funds for a portion of the bid price. The balance is usually due within a few weeks of the sale. You need some experience to buy properties at auction, so consider holding off until you have a few deals under your belt or have a partner who can show you the ropes.

Buy the Liens: At any time during the foreclosure process, you can buy the mortgage from the lender and finish the foreclosure. If the first mortgage is relatively small compared to the value of the property, it may be worthwhile to buy it. This method, of course, requires a lot of capital and experience.

In states that have a redemption period, many of the deals happen during that time. Remember that redemption is the right to purchase the property out of the foreclosure for the entire balance owed. The highest right of redemption is from the owner, borrower, or guarantor on the note. If none of these people redeem, the junior lien holders, who are in danger of being wiped out by the foreclosing senior lien holder, can redeem the property. Thus, if there are two mortgages on the property and the first mortgage holder is foreclosing, the second mortgage holder can redeem the property by paying what is owed on the first mortgage, plus late fees, court costs, and interest. The second mortgage holder then becomes the owner of the property. This process is technical and tricky and it often attracts crooks and scam artists who create phony liens in an attempt to redeem the property.

THE INTERNET

The number of people using the Internet is growing at an exponential rate. It used to be that only the more privileged had access. Now, people of all ages and levels of income have Internet access. Set up a Web site that advertises your service and any houses you have available for sale. Let other investors know what you have available on your site. You can register your domain name at <www.networksolutions.com>. Network Solutions and other providers have inexpensive hosting packages and simple on-line instructions for setting up a basic, yet professional-looking Web site.

GOVERNMENT-OWNED PROPERTIES

The federal government becomes the owner of tens of thousands of properties each year. Many can be purchased at good discounts, if you know how to find them.

FHA/VA "Repos"

Certain loan programs are guaranteed or insured by the federal government. The Federal Housing Administration (FHA), which operates under the Department of Housing and Urban Development (HUD), insures certain loans targeted at first-time homebuyers in lower income neighborhoods. The Veterans Administration (VA) guarantees similar loans for military personnel and their families. When these loans are in default, the government ends up with the properties.

Most of these properties are listed and sold through real estate agents. The property is first offered to potential owner-occupants in a bid process. When no suitable owner-occupant is found, the properties go on an extended listing, which is offered to everyone, including investors. You can place a bid on these properties with as little as $1,000 as earnest money, and if your bid is accepted, you have about 60 days to close. You can even extend that date a few weeks by paying a reasonable fee.

The bidding process is difficult and you need a savvy real estate agent to help you along. As you may have guessed, the great thing about the HUD/VA process is that you have a long time to close and are only required to risk $1,000 in earnest money. However, the HUD/VA contract has no "weasel clauses," so you will lose your earnest money if you fail to close.

Furthermore, the HUD/VA contract is not assignable, so you have to do a double closing to flip the property to another investor. If you get the property at the right price, 60 days is more than enough time to make things happen.

IRS/GSA Program

When a taxpayer is in default of his income tax obligations, the Internal Revenue Service (IRS) may file a lien in the county in which the taxpayer lives. If he owns real estate, the lien attaches to the property. The taxpayer cannot sell or refinance the property without settling the debt with the IRS.

If a property that has an IRS lien is foreclosed, the IRS has 180 days after the foreclosure sale to redeem the property. The IRS loses its rights against the taxpayer's house if it does not redeem the property.

The Government Services Administration (GSA) and the IRS have developed a program under which investors can underwrite the purchase of the property. An investor submits a minimum guaranteed bid that is acceptable to the IRS. Once a bid is accepted, the IRS will redeem the property, and then the GSA will place the property up for public sale. The investor who placed the minimum-accepted bid will automatically be the first bidder for the GSA sale. If no one else outbids the investor at the GSA's public sale, the investor gets to purchase the property. For more information about properties available, call the GSA at 800-421-7848 or subscribe to <www.foreclosures-usa.com>.

Key Points to Remember

- Find the motivated seller and you find a bargain property.
- Learn how to farm neighborhoods.
- Use multiple marketing approaches.
- Use your business card and your contacts to get referral business.
- Learn how to work the foreclosure business.

CHAPTER 4

Analyzing a Good Deal

It takes experience to recognize a profitable deal. Of course, experience usually comes from making lots of mistakes. Use this book to learn from our mistakes so that you don't lose money the hard way. Be aware of local and regional market trends, but do not be paralyzed by these trends. The concept of flipping properties works in every market, in every city, whether the market is hot or in the pits.

PICK THE RIGHT NEIGHBORHOODS

You can flip houses in any neighborhood, but stay with the low- to middle-priced areas that are 15 to 50 years old. Don't buy in gang-ridden, high-crime areas at first, for your market for resale is very small. Buy in working-class areas where housing is affordable and desirable. Beware of the so-called median price or some figure that real estate agents use. This figure may be skewed by higher-priced newly constructed homes. Furthermore, stay with the populated areas that are in high demand. You can make a profit in other areas, but this approach takes more experience and involves more risk. As a beginner, follow these guidelines and you can't go wrong.

Starter Homes

Concentrate on purchasing starter homes at first. These homes are the least expensive single-family homes (and possibly condominiums) in each area. Usually they will be two- or three-bedroom ranch-style houses. If possible, choose an area close to where you live. Staying close to home means you will know the neighborhood and its current trends. The neighborhood does not need to be in a location where you would choose to live, but it should not be in a slum, either. If you are not sure about an area, check the local police departments for available crime statistics. Other resources include the local chamber of commerce, planning department, real estate agents, and census reports. You should also subscribe to (and read!) local and regional newspapers.

PICK THE RIGHT KIND OF HOUSES

Choose houses that are consistent with the neighborhood. For example, don't buy one-bedroom houses unless there are several in the area. If you are in a warm, humid climate, make sure the house has air-conditioning. If every house in the area has two bedrooms, don't buy a five-bedroom home; it may be overpriced for the area. You are always better off buying the cheapest house in a better neighborhood than the highest-priced house in a poor neighborhood.

Functional Obsolescence

Be wary of poorly designed houses. It is OK to buy a house that needs work or remodeling, but don't buy houses that have basic design problems, such as five bedrooms and only one bath and no tub. Beware of the odd man out house on the block. For example, if every house has a garage and the subject house does not, you could have a problem when you try to sell it. If each house on the block was built in the 1950s, don't buy the old farmhouse that was built in 1890, unless you plan on demolishing it. Finally, keep in mind that the house may eventually be purchased by a retail buyer with FHA or VA financing (the Federal Housing Administration insures FHA loans and the Veterans Administration guarantees VA loans). The house must conform to strict guidelines for the government to guarantee the loan. You can learn what these guidelines are by contacting your local HUD or VA office and by talking to appraisers in your area.

ESTABLISH VALUE

It is extremely important to establish the value of a property prior to making an offer. You must know value so you can determine what you should offer in your purchase contract. Base your offer on what the house will sell for after necessary repairs. Remember to learn the area first, and buy in your farm area (see Chapter 3) when possible. Always take a conservative approach until you gain experience in dealing in a particular market. Start with a few neighborhoods within a subdivision that contains similar houses, for dealing with similar houses makes price comparisons much easier.

Using Professional Help

An expensive, but accurate way to determine the value of a home is to hire a licensed appraiser. The appraisal will cost you around $300. This amount is cheap compared to what you could potentially lose, but can be costly if you are making multiple offers. It may be worthwhile to pay an appraiser on your first purchases to verify your assumptions of value (but not until you have the properties under contract). In addition, follow him as he inspects the property and ask a lot of questions to learn how he arrives at his figures.

Basically, a licensed appraiser looks at the three most similar houses in the vicinity that have sold recently. He then compares square footage and other attributes (see the sample appraisal form in Appendix C). The number of bedrooms and baths, age of the property, improvements, physical condition, and the presence of a garage will affect the price, but square footage is usually the most important factor. As you might expect, there are exceptions to this rule. For example, the style of house, its location and proximity to main roads, and whether it has a view or beach access will greatly affect the value. Of course, you probably will not be flipping many beachfront properties. For the most part, however, if you leave these issues aside, square footage, number of bedrooms and baths, and physical condition are the most relevant factors. Also, keep in mind that bedrooms and baths on the main level add more value than bedrooms and baths in a basement or attic.

Doing Your Own Appraisal

Doing an appraisal yourself is not that difficult. You need to access information about houses sold recently. Until now, access to this information was limited to licensed real estate agents through a computer database called the Multiple Listing Service (MLS). In today's Information Age, this data is available through various channels, such as the county tax assessor, the Internet, or paid providers (a list of these sites can be found in Appendix E). Armed with information about properties sold in the area, you can drive by these houses and compare them with the subject property. You will not be able to see the inside, so you need to adjust your numbers a bit. Also, public records may have inaccurate information about square footage, additions or number of beds and baths, and basement versus above-ground living space. In addition, public records do not offer much detail, and the property may have been improved or expanded after it was built.

All of these variables aside, you can still assess the style of property, whether it has a garage, its general condition and appearance. Only look at houses sold in the area within the past six months. Try to acquire information about the type of financing on the house, because terms can influence the sales price. For example, an owner-carry sale (one in which the seller takes all or part of the purchase price in the form of a note) at an inflated price should not be considered in your figures, for these prices tend to be artificially high.

Keep in mind that seasons affect sales prices. Most people prefer to buy in the summer when their children are out of school. Additionally, if you are in a resort area, prices may fluctuate drastically between the summer and the winter.

Comparable Sales

A practical but less accurate way to establish value is by asking a real estate agent for comparable sales or comps. If the property is listed or you are using a buyer's agent (see Chapter 3), he will gladly provide this information free of charge. Some listing agents will have preprepared a written comparative market analysis (CMA) for the property. You cannot always rely on the MLS information about the inside, for agent's property descriptions tend to be exaggerated. Furthermore, the information on the comparable properties that the agent gives you may only contain the ones he wants you to see. The lesson here is to never rely solely on an agent's comps or CMAs, but do your own due diligence.

If the property was refinanced in the past year or so, take a look at the seller's appraisal. Keep in mind that some appraisers will inflate the value of the property if they are in close with the mortgage broker handling the refinancing. This practice is legal within limits because the appraiser is required to determine property value based on certain guidelines. A seller wants a high appraisal, so her appraiser will utilize the highest comps. A person fighting a high property tax assessment can instruct the appraiser to find low (while still conforming) comparable sales.

WHAT IS A GOOD DEAL?

There is no exact formula for a good deal that works in every neighborhood and in every market. It takes experience to recognize the potential in a real estate transaction. The catch-22 is that lack of experience will make it harder to recognize a good deal. More often than not, investors pay too much for properties. People who buy for speculation often get hurt financially because they are depending on factors beyond their control, such as the market, the neighborhood, favorable zoning, or other long-term factors. As a property flipper, do not be concerned with factors beyond your control. *You must make your profit when you purchase, so buy it right!*

Discount in Price

This may sound redundant, but don't make the mistake of paying too much for a property. Believe it or not, most investors know what they want to pay for a property, but are afraid to ask. They are afraid that the seller will be offended and refuse to negotiate any further. A seller will only be offended if you ask in the wrong way (see Chapter 5).

Pay Full Price and Still Profit

In Chapter 1, we discouraged acting as a real estate speculator. However, as a dealer you can flip properties to speculators. In certain inner-city neighborhoods, developers and speculators are willing to pay full price and more for properties—not for the house, but for the land value. Often homeowners in the path of a new development are stubborn and refuse to sell to these developers and speculators. These homeowners may, however, sell to you! Thus, you can sign a purchase contract for full price and flip it to a developer for more money. In some areas of the country, new developments are sold out before the houses are built. This lack of supply may increase the value of properties in the development by as much as 20 percent by the time all the houses are finished. With as little as $1,000 down, you can sign a contract with the developer to purchase a home before it is built. By the time the house is complete, you can find an owner-occupant to buy the house from you in a double closing. This is one of the few times you will act as both a dealer and retailer. ■

Presumably, you will be starting out as a scout or dealer, so you need to establish the wholesale price for a property. As with any other business, there is a wholesale price and a retail price. Find out what kind of discount the retailers are looking for and you will have a starting point. For example, a retailer may tell you he is willing to pay 80 percent of the property's market value. Subtract from that discounted price the estimated cost of repairs (as we will discuss in Chapter 9), leaving a healthy margin for error. Then subtract your profit in the deal. Your profit may be anywhere from $1,000 to $5,000, depending on the price of the property and your marketplace.

Don't Be Greedy: When figuring in your profit, don't expect too much. Many amateur and some experienced, albeit foolish, investors expect more profit than they deserve out of a deal. You must be realistic. If you want to sell a property quickly to another investor who will do a lot of work, you can't expect to make as much as he will. While it is possible to negotiate a great price and make a killing, remember that most deals do not have enough room for two investors to make a killing.

Remember to Add in Your Profit: The corollary to don't be greedy is to remember to make your offer with two investors in mind. A lot of beginning dealers forget that there must be enough profit in the deal for both themselves and the retailer to make money. Thus, you must offer the seller the wholesale price, less your anticipated profit.

Let's summarize the price you are looking for as a dealer:

	Retail Price	*established by appraisal and/or comps*
multiplied by	.8 Discount	*established by local property retailers*
less	Repairs	*estimated conservatively*
less	Your Fee	*$1,000 to $5,000*
	------------------	
equals	**Your Purchase Price**	

The Retailer's Bid

It is relatively easy to find a starting point as a dealer, for you simply ask the retailer what he is willing to pay you. Thus, being a retailer takes a little more experience in estimating the following factors:

- Market value of the property after resale
- Acquisition and financing costs
- Labor and material costs (and cost overruns)
- Time required to complete repairs, weather factors, and availability of labor
- Estimated time on the market
- Time involved for supervising construction
- Real estate agent commissions and other sales costs

There is no magic formula that works in every market in every neighborhood and for every house. In our market (Denver, Colorado), we deal in middle- to lower-priced homes, which are very easy to sell. Thus, we can buy properties at 85 percent of the market value or more and still make a nice profit. In slower markets, such as Hawaii, Upstate New York, and central Pennsylvania, properties may sit for six months or more on the MLS; this means you must purchase properties at a deep, deep discount, at as little as 50 percent. On the contrary, other higher-end properties, which also take longer to sell, must be purchased at a more substantial discount.

Our recommendation is to flip a few properties first, then review the numbers on those properties with the retailers who sold them to the owner-occupants. After reviewing a dozen or so deals with several retailers, you will get a feel for what kind of discount is necessary.

After establishing the retail price, the appropriate discount, repairs, and your profit, you finally arrive at your offering price, right? *Wrong!* This price is the maximum you can afford to pay. Leave enough room in the equation for the seller's counter-offer. This discussion brings us to the next, topic, which is . . . negotiating!

Key Points to Remember

- Pick the right neighborhoods.
- Learn how to establish value.
- Find out what other investors are willing to pay for properties and find deals that suit their needs.

CHAPTER 5

The Art of Negotiating the Deal

Negotiating the right price and/or terms for your properties is the most important part of the profit-making process. Many people are afraid to negotiate, or are inept at the negotiating process. Other so-called investors pay too much for a property and then are left with no way to make a profit other than the "greater fool" theory. Learn to negotiate a good purchase price quickly, or you will face a tough road ahead in becoming an investor.

DEAL ONLY WITH MOTIVATED SELLERS

The biggest mistake you can make is negotiating with someone who is not highly motivated to sell. Once in a while, you will run across the garage sale seller; i.e., someone without a clue about the value of his property. These opportunities are rare and will not make you a living. Rather than taking advantage of ignorant people, deal with people who need to sell and want to sell quickly.

FIND OUT WHAT THE SELLER WANTS

Many novice investors spend countless hours researching the property, the needed repairs, the taxes, and other information without first finding out the seller's motivation. This mistake relates to the rule about never dealing with unmotivated people. Once you have established that someone is motivated, dig deeper. Find out exactly what makes this seller tick. Why does she need to sell? When does she need to sell by? Is price more important than terms? What will she do with the proceeds? These are questions you need to get answered before you even consider making an offer or leaving your house to see a property.

Don't be too concerned with the physical aspects of the property when talking with a seller on the phone. Your goal is to determine whether the seller is motivated enough to make you a deal.

Don't jump right in with the tough questions that may offend the seller. Start by asking a few questions about the property. Talk about the weather, the sports teams, how much you hate politicians, etc. When you sense the seller is opening up a bit, ask her the following questions:

- "Why are you selling?"
- "How long have your owned the property?"
- "What did you pay for it when you bought it?"
- "When do you need to sell it by?"
- "Have you listed it with a real estate agent? Why/Why not?"
- "What are your plans after you sell?"
- "After paying all the closing costs and paying off your loan, what is the minimum amount of cash you need in your pocket?
- "What will you do with the proceeds from the sale of your house?"

- "If I were to close in a week and pay all cash, what is the very best you can do in terms of price?"

Continue to develop your phone skills and try experimenting with new questions. You need to communicate in a way that works with your personality. No one can tell you all the perfect things to say for each situation. Just be yourself; develop rapport and zone in on what the seller needs. The best salesperson is the one who finds what his customer needs and presents his product in a way that fulfills that need. Successful investors are essentially problem solvers. Problem solvers are among the highest paid individuals in the world. The problems homeowners face may seem to them insurmountable. With experience and practice, however, you will learn many approaches to solving their problems. It is just a matter of time until you, the investor, will earn a profit while helping a homeowner solve her problem in an ethical way.

Just for practice, record your telephone conversations with motivated sellers (be discreet, however—it is illegal in some states!). Use these recordings to improve your sales pitch. Track your results and you will soon find an effective approach for making your calls.

LET THE SELLER MAKE YOU AN OFFER

Most novice investors make the foolish mistake of always making the first offer. In some circumstances, this approach may be appropriate or desirable. If your offer is too low, the seller may be offended. Let the seller make the first move. "Mr. Seller, what is the best deal you can offer me on this property?" This statement puts the pressure on him. He may be afraid he'll drive you away if he asks too much. Whatever he offers, you ask him to do better. Henry Kissinger was the master of this technique. He would routinely send back proposals without reading them, saying, "You can do better." Get the seller to go as low as possible, then negotiate from there.

LEAVE YOURSELF ROOM TO RENEGOTIATE

Once you get a contract accepted at the price you like, it may still be too much. Leave room for error or for things you overlooked. Always have an inspection clause in your contract (see Chapter 6) that allows you to dicker with the seller and to renegotiate if necessary. Don't misunderstand—we are not advocating that you beat up people after you agree on a price. However, sometimes you will discover problems with the property that were unknown to either party or that the seller conveniently forgot to tell you about. As a real estate agent friend used to say, "All sellers are storytellers!"

PRICE ISN'T EVERYTHING

As we discussed previously, it is essential to know what motivates the seller. Some sellers want the highest price, but many just want their problems solved quickly.

Offer a Fast Closing

Offering a fast closing with few contingencies will often perk up the seller's ears. If the seller says, "A real estate agent told me the property is worth more," you respond with, "Does the real estate agent have a buyer ready to close next week?" Sometimes offering a contract with no contingencies is your strongest offer, especially when dealing with real estate agents (see a later section in this chapter). Of course, a real estate contract with no contingencies is risky, for you lose your earnest money deposit if you fail to purchase the property (see contract contingencies in Chapter 6).

Purchase "Subject to" the Existing Mortgage

When the retailer quotes you the appropriate discount he wants, he is including the cost of financing the property. Most retailers use credit lines and/or conventional bank financing to purchase properties. These loans have certain costs associated with them, which reduce the net profit in the deal. Whether you are a dealer or a retailer, you can save money by avoiding these new loan costs, thus offering the seller a higher price (or more net cash in his pocket).

Chances are, the seller has an existing loan on the property. Offer the seller the cash difference between the purchase price and his loan balance. At the closing, you take the title subject to the existing mortgage (see Chapter 2 for a discussion on subject to transfers). You make the monthly payments directly to his lender and pay off the balance of the mortgage when the property is sold to the retail buyer. Even if you are buying the property with subject to conditions as a dealer, you can pass these savings on to the retailer who buys the property from you. Another benefit of the subject to transaction is that it allows you to close without a third-party lender, which translates to a faster closing.

The Split-Funded Sale

A seller you are negotiating with may own her property outright or may have a very small mortgage. Thus, the seller may receive more cash from closing than she needs (which you have already established by asking good questions). If this is the case, offer to split-fund the purchase price. Split-funding means you will pay her "some now, some later." Offer to pay her 20 percent at closing, followed by another 20 percent in 60 days, and the balance in six months. Be creative with your offers and conserve your cash whenever possible.

Multiple Offers

When you make an offer, the seller has two choices: Take it or leave it. When you make two alternative offers, the seller has more choices. For example, you can offer him all cash and a 30-day closing or a split-funded purchase that closes next week. In some cases, it doesn't even occur to the seller that he doesn't need to accept either offer!

NEVER OFFER A CONCESSION WITHOUT RECEIVING SOMETHING IN RETURN

This strategy is one of the most underused in the negotiation game. If the seller asks for more money, you ask for more time. If the seller asks for a shorter closing date, you ask for the appliances. If he wants a higher price, you ask for more time to close. Never give a concession without getting something in return.

DEALING WITH REAL ESTATE AGENTS

Real estate agents have access to a valuable source of potential deals for the investor—the Multiple Listing Service (MLS).

Unfortunately, real estate agents have a monopoly on this information, so they may be a necessary part of an investor's game plan. Some local boards of REALTORS® have begun offering affiliate memberships to non-REALTORS® to permit limited access to the MLS. Check with your local board to see if this type of membership is available.

Dealing with real estate agents can be difficult as an investor. Agents prefer homebuyers with cash for down payments. They also prefer to work with buyers who have good credit and conventional buying power. The agent's priority is getting a commission with as little hassle as possible. Most agents have never conducted a creative real estate transaction with an investor. These agents are not very receptive to unusual offers. Most agents equate a nothing down offer with a buyer who is not serious.

Offer Reasonable Earnest Money

You cannot present an offer with a $50 earnest money deposit and expect an agent to take you seriously. Expect to pay at least $500 to $1,000 (depending on the purchase price) earnest money to get the agent's (and seller's) attention. Offer more earnest money when presenting an all-cash offer. If you are concerned with losing your earnest money, consider using a promissory note (see Chapter 6).

Offer a Short Closing Date

Another way to get an agent's attention is to offer a fast closing. Nothing makes an agent more excited than the thought of a commission check in ten days. When deciding between two offers, the agent will usually advise his client to accept an offer with more earnest money and a faster closing over a higher-priced offer.

Insist on Presenting Creative Offers in Person

When you present an offer to an agent, he then presents it to the seller on your behalf. If you present a creative offer, the agent will not represent your offer to the seller in your same enthusiastic fashion. As stated previously, agents do not like creative offers; they like conventional offers from solid buyers. If you want the owner to understand all the benefits of your offer, insist on personally presenting the offer to the seller.

Appeal to the Agent's Greed Factor

Let's face it, real estate agents are in the game to make money, just like people in other businesses. If you offer the agent an opportunity to make money out of the transaction, you will get his cooperation. If you present an offer that does not provide enough cash to pay the agent, then he has no reason to cooperate with you. For example, if you present a nothing down offer on a listed property, how will the agent receive a commission? You must include a means to pay the agent, even if you pay him out of your own pocket.

Do Your Own Comps

Sometimes you will deal with the opposite of an uncooperative agent—an overzealous agent. Be suspicious of an agent who tells you what a deal you are getting on a property. If it is such a good deal, why didn't he buy it? Do not trust him to determine the property's value. Do your own assessment of value. Remember, the agent is looking out for his commission, not for your financial well-being.

Fax Preliminary Offers First

Technically speaking, all offers presented by agents must be made on state-approved contracts. Do not waste time filling out a contract offer until you have preliminary approval. Most agents are willing to present any written offer to the seller. Simply summarize your offer in writing and fax it to the listing agent (see sample form in Appendix C). Once you have an oral approval, take the time to fill out a contract and deliver an earnest money check. *Never* put up earnest money until the offer is accepted! Fax the offer with a copy of an earnest money check with originals to be delivered "upon acceptance of contract."

Don't Be Bullied by Uncooperative Agents

Do not be afraid to stand up to an uncooperative agent. Some agents are unethical and will refuse to present your offer. These agents may lie, telling you that your offer was rejected when, in fact, it was never presented. If you suspect the listing agent is lying, do not be afraid to go over his head to the managing broker of the office. If the managing broker is uncooperative, deal directly with the seller (unless, of course, you are also an agent). Be polite, but firm, and do not hesitate to report any unethical behavior to your state's Department of Real Estate.

Key Points to Remember

- Only negotiate with motivated sellers.
- Ask the right questions to determine the seller's level of motivation.
- Negotiate a discount in price and/or a subject to deal.
- Learn how to deal with real estate agents.

CHAPTER 6

Putting It in Writing

BASIC CONTRACT PRINCIPLES

Real estate contracts are based on common contract principles, so it is important that you understand the basics of contract law.

Offer, Counteroffer, and Acceptance

The process begins with an offer. A contract is formed when an offer is made and accepted. In most states standardized contracts drafted in the form of offers are used by real estate agents and attorneys. The offer is usually signed by the buyer (the offeror) and contains all the material terms of a contract, with the exception of the seller's signature.

The basic building block of a contract is mutual agreement. The contract is not binding until the seller accepts, creating a meeting of the minds. An acceptance is made if the offeree (the seller, in this case) agrees to the exact terms of the offer. If the offer comes back to the offeror with changes, there is no binding contract, but rather a counteroffer. Thus, if the seller signs the purchase contract, but changes the closing date to five days sooner, there is no agreement. Furthermore, if the offer is not accepted in the time frame and manner set forth by the offeror, then there is no contract. For example, if the contract specifies that acceptance must be made by facsimile, an acceptance by telephone call or mail will not suffice.

Unilateral Contract versus Bilateral Contract

A real estate sales contract is a bilateral or two-way agreement. The seller agrees to sell, and the purchaser agrees to buy. Compare this agreement with an option; an option is a unilateral or one-way agreement by which the seller is obligated to sell, but the purchaser is not obligated to buy. On the other hand, if the purchaser on a bilateral contract refuses to buy, he can be held liable for damages.

A contract with a contingency is similar to a purchase option. A purchase option gives the buyer the exclusive right to buy, but does not obligate that buyer to do so. Many contracts contain contingencies (see the contingency section in this chapter), which, if not met, result in the termination of the contract. In essence, a bilateral contract with a contingency in favor of the purchaser turns a bilateral contract into an option because it gives the purchaser an out if he decides not to purchase the property. Though the two are not legally the same, an option and a bilateral purchase contract with a contingency yield the same practical result.

Basic Legal Requirements of a Real Estate Contract

Several basic requirements must be present to make a real estate contract valid:

Mutual Agreement: As stated earlier, there must be a mutual agreement or a meeting of the minds.

In Writing: With few exceptions, a contract for purchase and sale of real estate must be in writing to be enforceable. Thus, if a buyer makes an offer in writing and the seller accepts orally, then backs out, the buyer is out of luck.

Identify the Parties: The contract must identify the parties. Although not legally required, a contract commonly sets forth full names and middle initials (this helps the title company prepare the title commitment). If one of the parties is a corporation, it should so state (e.g., North American Land Acquisitions, Inc., a Nevada corporation).

Identify the Property: The contract must identify the property. Although not required, a legal description should be included. A vague description such as "my lakefront home" may not be specific enough to create a binding contract.

Purchase Price: The contract must state the purchase price of the property or a reasonably ascertainable figure (e.g., "appraised value as determined by ABC Appraisers, Inc.").

Consideration: A contract must have consideration to be enforceable. Consideration is the benefit, interest, or value that induces a promise; it is the glue that binds a contract. The amount of consideration is not important, but rather whether there is consideration at all. It is common for a contract to read that "ten dollars and other good and valuable consideration has been paid and received." Consideration need not be cash; it can be property, a promissory note, or an agreement to perform services.

Signatures: A contract must be signed to be enforceable. The party signing must be of legal age and sound mind. A notary's signature or witness is not required. A facsimile signature is usually acceptable, so long as the contract states that facsimile signatures are valid.

EARNEST MONEY

A buyer will usually put up earnest money to bind the contract and show that he is a serious buyer. Most sellers ask for the earnest money deposit because they are afraid of tying up the property and rejecting other potential buyers.

How Much Earnest Money Is Necessary?

The law requires no specific amount of earnest money. In fact, if the transaction involves the buyer simply taking over a loan and the property has no equity, it may be appropriate for the seller to give the buyer consideration. When you are buying, you want to put down as little as possible ($50 to $500); when selling, you should get as much as possible ($1,000 to $5,000). Of course, the amount of earnest money will depend on the motivation of the parties, seller's representation by real estate professionals, the purchase price, and the length of time until closing.

Promissory Note

If you are afraid of losing your earnest money as a buyer, you may consider offering a promissory note as earnest money. A seller may be reluctant to accept a promissory note rather than cash because it requires the seller to sue you to collect on the note if you default. As a compromise, you can structure the contract so that the seller receives a promissory note as earnest money that is paid in full after the property is inspected, but prior to closing.

Who Should Hold the Earnest Money?

A big issue for the parties is who should hold the earnest money deposit in escrow. Theoretically, the escrow agent (the person holding the earnest money) must release the funds to the seller if the buyer breaches and to the buyer if the contract is canceled. However, the escrow agent will not usually release the funds without the permission of both parties, even in the face of a clear breach or cancellation. Furthermore, if the escrow agent is the listing broker, she may side with the seller and not release the money (the listing broker has an incentive to keep the earnest money because his listing agreement usually gives him part of the forfeited earnest money deposit as a commission). The seller would obviously prefer to have his broker hold escrow, while the buyer would want a neutral or buyer-friendly title or escrow company to hold the earnest money.

CONTINGENCIES

As mentioned earlier, a contingency is a clause in a contract that must be satisfied for the contract to be complete. If the contingencies are not satisfied, the contract terminates and the parties go their merry ways. The contract will usually provide that in the event of termination, the buyer is entitled to a return of his earnest money.

Inspection Contingency

Most standard real estate contracts contain an inspection clause, which gives the buyer a certain amount of time to inspect the premises. After he inspects the premises, he should provide the seller with a list of potential problems or defects and give the seller a chance to remedy these problems, adjust the purchase price, or choose to terminate the agreement. Most standard inspection clauses place the burden of inspecting and disapproving on the buyer. Thus, his failure to timely inspect and object will result in his waiver of this contingency. Used properly, the inspection clause will allow a buyer to terminate a contract that was signed hastily and later turns out to be a bad deal.

Inspection clauses can be written a variety of ways. As the buyer, of course, you would prefer a more liberal, subjective approach, permitting you to perform the inspection without a licensed professional and disapprove of items in any manner you wish. However, you cannot use the inspection clause in an arbitrary fashion to cancel a purchase contract, for there is an implied duty of good faith on your part to deal fairly.

Loan Approval Contingency

Virtually every standard real estate contract gives the buyer a contingency to find a loan to purchase the property. The buyer cannot simply sit back and say, "Oh well, I couldn't get a loan." The buyer is obligated to make reasonable efforts to make applications to various lenders and comply with the lenders' demands for proof of employment, copies of tax returns, etc. The loan contingency will usually state a certain date by which the buyer must present the seller with a copy of a written loan commitment from the lender.

Marketable Title

The contract will usually provide that it is contingent upon proof of a marketable title by a certain date. The seller is usually required to provide the buyer a copy of a title report or a title commitment showing that the title is insurable. Even if the title report shows problems with the title, the contract is still in force if the seller can cure the problems before the closing and deliver a marketable title. For example, the existence of a lien or judgment is not fatal, because it can be satisfied by the seller from the proceeds at the closing.

BREACH OF CONTRACT

What happens when one party breaches the agreement? There are many legal implications of a party breaching a contract, but it is more important that you understand the practical side (for real estate litigation is usually a costly matter that should be avoided).

Buyer's Remedies for Breach

If the seller breaches the contract by failing to close the title, the buyer has three legal remedies:

1. Sue for specific performance.
2. Sue for damages.
3. Sue for return of the earnest money.

Sue for Specific Performance: Specific performance is a remedy granted by a court, which forces the seller to sell to the buyer. If the property is unique and you feel like spending $10,000 in legal fees, then you will probably win the lawsuit if the seller refuses to close title. If the seller refused to close because he got greedy and found another buyer, you can record a copy of your contract or an affidavit (called a memorandum of agreement) in the public records. This will create a cloud on the title, which will alarm other buyers and title companies. Obviously, recording a contract or memorandum is a much more inexpensive and practical approach. You will find a sample memorandum of agreement form in Appendix C.

Sue for Damages: If the property was to be purchased at a discount or was intended to be resold for a profit, you may be able to sue for your loss of potential profit. Of course, loss of profit is difficult to prove, for it is not clear exactly what price you could have sold it for, how long it would have taken you, and how much it would have cost you in repairs. Even if you could prove this by expert testimony, the lawsuit could cost you $10,000 in legal fees.

Sue for Return of the Earnest Money: If the seller refuses to close and blames you for the incident, you may simply have to sue to get back your earnest money. Most local small-claims courts can hear these types of cases, so long as the amount of earnest money involved is small (most small-claims courts will only hear cases involving controversies of less than $2,000 to $3,000). If the earnest money is more (shame on you for giving so much!), you will need to proceed in the next highest court that usually conducts somewhat informal trials, similar to small-claims court. You may need a lawyer to assist you with the court procedure.

Seller's Remedies for Buyer's Breach

As you can see, the seller, who has title, is in a better position than the buyer. The seller has three legal remedies for the buyer's breach of contract:

1. Keep the buyer's earnest money.
2. Sue for damages.
3. Sue for specific performance.

Keep the Buyer's Earnest Money: The seller's best remedy is his ability to keep the buyer's earnest money. If the contract calls for the seller to keep the earnest money as liquidated damages, then the seller can keep it, even if he sells the property to someone else for full price. In most cases, the buyer will walk away and cut his losses, especially if the earnest money is not significant. If the buyer objects and the money is held in escrow, then the seller and/or buyer will have to go to court to battle it out.

Even if the buyer is in breach, he may be able to argue that it is unjust for the seller to keep the earnest money. This argument is not usually successful, unless the amount of money is large and the buyer's breach was insignificant (e.g., the buyer was one day late in obtaining his loan commitment and the seller declared the contract in default). In the case of forfeiting an earnest money deposit, it may be cheaper for both parties to settle out of court.

Sue for Damages: If the contract does not limit the seller's remedy to the retention of the earnest money, the seller can also sue the buyer for his actual damages. For example, if the property is in the northeast and the seller took the property off the market for the summer, he may now be in a position where he must hold the property through the winter at his expense. If the seller can quantify his damages, he may be able to sue the buyer for failing to close. Of course, this can be an expensive lawsuit, but at least the seller will have leverage if the buyer will not agree to release the earnest money deposit.

Sue for Specific Performance: The seller can also sue for specific performance to force the buyer to purchase the property.

This may be futile, for the buyer may not be financially able to purchase the property. It may also be very expensive in terms of legal fees and court costs.

DRAFTING THE OFFER

The contract provided in Appendix C is fine if you are dealing directly with a seller. It contains all the necessary contingencies you need to protect yourself. If you are making an offer through a real estate agent, however, you must use the standard form. You cannot use your own contract when making an offer through a real estate agent.

The following is a checklist of items to look for when you are buying. Some of these clauses may be found in some form or another in the standard real estate contract that is used in your area.

The Right to Assign

As the buyer, you want to have the right to assign your contract (see Chapter 2). In the absence of a statement claiming otherwise, a contract is usually assignable. By placing your name as buyer with the words, *and/or assigns,* you automatically give yourself that right. However, if the preprinted portion of the contract contains a provision forbidding assignment without the seller's permission, you must cross out that provision.

Inclusions and Exclusions

Most real estate contracts have a clause that specifies what personal property is included in or excluded from the sale. Sellers and buyers often forget to specify certain items, which leads to arguments at closing. A few appliances could be worth $500 or more to you (or cost $500 out of your pocket if you have to replace them). As the buyer, you would prefer the clause, "anything not specifically excluded will be included, whether or not affixed to the property or structures."

Earnest Money

As the buyer, your preference is for earnest money "to be held in escrow by an escrow agent or a title company of the buyer's choice." Never let the seller hold the escrow. When selling, do just the opposite; keep the earnest money in your account of a title company of your choosing.

Cash Required at the Closing

What happens if you are assuming or taking title subject to an existing loan and it turns out that the actual balance of the loan is less than the seller thought? This may mean you have to come up with extra cash at the closing. To prevent such a disaster, insert the clause:

> If the actual loan balance is less than as stated herein, the purchase price shall be reduced to reflect the difference; if the actual loan balance is more than as stated herein, then buyer's required cash payment shall be reduced accordingly.

New Loan Contingency

If you intend to obtain a bank loan to purchase the property, you should include this contingency in the contract. The loan contingency clause has been interpreted broadly by courts as putting the obligation on the buyer to make reasonable attempts to obtain a loan. Lenders are very aggressive these days, so virtually anyone can get a loan. The issue really becomes how many points and how high of an interest rate you want to pay. The buyer should have a clause that reads similar to the following:

Buyer is not required to accept a loan with an interest rate of higher than _____ percent over ____ years and payments exceeding _____/month and buyer is not required to accept any loan that requires more than $_____ in points, closing, and/or other fees.

Waiver of Escrow Balance

Most lenders escrow taxes and insurance from the borrower each month in an impound account. Typically, the buyer reimburses the seller for the amount in escrow with the lender when assuming the seller's loan. Whether you take title subject to or assume an existing loan, insert the phrase, "seller agrees to waive tax and insurance escrows held with lender." Using this clause will help to avoid your having to come up with a couple hundred dollars in cash at closing to reimburse the seller for an escrow account, the proceeds of which you may not see for several years.

Owner Financing

If the purchase consists of some owner financing, the buyer should look for the following:

- The loan should contain no due-on-sale clause (so the property can be resold to another investor on owner-carry terms); and
- The loan should be nonrecourse, which means that it prevents a judgment against the buyer if the loan is in default. The operative language is: "Seller's sole recourse in case of default shall be against the property and there shall be no personal recourse against the borrower."

Appraisal Provision

If the contract calls for an appraisal contingency, the buyer prefers one that does not require a licensed appraiser. This will give the buyer an out if he can find a local real estate agent who will vouch that the property will not appraise.

The Right to Choose the Closing Agent

There's an old saying about marriage that goes something like this: "Choose your spouse carefully, for this one decision can lead to 90 percent of your happiness or misery." For real estate transactions, substitute the words *closing agent* for *spouse*. We cannot tell you how much heartache and aggravation you will save by using a closing agent who understands the double closing process. As the buyer, insist on the right to choose the title or escrow company so that you remain in control. If the property is listed with an agent, he may have his preference of title or escrow company. Offer to pay the full closing fee (usually about $250) for the right to choose—it is well worth it!

Right to Extend the Closing Date

Most contracts call for a date certain for closing. If the buyer is not ready to close, the seller can hold him in default. Here are some tips for buying time:

- Make the closing date "on or about" rather than "on or before." What does on or about mean? This is up to the judge, but we guarantee it will buy you some time (of course, when selling, make your closing date "on or before").
- Have the right to extend the closing date if it is not your fault: "Said date may be extended an additional fifteen (15) days if lender requires additional documentation, paperwork, or actions from the buyer and said delay is not due to the fault of the buyer."
- Have the right to extend for 30 days by paying the seller the equivalent of one month's mortgage payment.

Possession

As the buyer, you want possession of the property concurrent with the closing. If the sellers are living there, make sure that you have the right to charge them a hefty daily rent if they are in possession after closing. If the contract calls for allowing the sellers to remain in possession after closing, consider holding back some of the proceeds to ensure you will get possession when you need it.

Many sellers underestimate the time they need to move, and the longer they are in possession, the more money it costs you.

Also, the contract should state that the property be left "broom clean and free from all debris." A cleaning crew and a hauling truck could cost you several hundred dollars if the seller leaves a lot of unwanted property behind.

How to Draft the Contract When You Sell

Most of the discussion here involves drafting a contract slanted in your favor when buying. When selling a property to another investor, you should use the standard real estate contract that the real estate agents use in your area. This will make financing easier for the buyer, for banks and title companies are familiar with the form. Several words of advice: Limit the inspection contingency to 48 hours, have a short closing date, and get as much earnest money as possible. A serious investor should have no objection to inspecting the property immediately, putting up $2,000 or more as earnest money, and closing within a few weeks.

Seller's Remedy Limited to Earnest Money

Unless stated otherwise, the seller can keep your earnest money and sue you for breach. Give small earnest money deposits and use the phrase, "upon default, seller's sole and only remedy shall be to retain buyer's earnest money." If the seller insists on a larger earnest money deposit, insert a phrase that entitles you to interest at the highest rate permitted by law on your money. That way, the seller will be less likely to hold on to your earnest money for six months while you sue him to get it back.

Weasel Clauses

A buyer wants as many contingencies or weasel clauses as possible. If the buyer can get out of a contract without breaching, then he is entitled to his earnest money. The less earnest money you put up, the less you need a weasel clause. If you do need a weasel clause, here are a few favorites:

- "This agreement is subject to inspection and approval of the property by the buyer in writing prior to _____."
- "This agreement is subject to attorney approval within seventy-two (72) hours."

Access to the Property before Closing

If you intend to flip the property to another investor, you may need access to the property before the closing. If you intend to rehab the property, you have to get access to obtain contractor's bids. Try the following clause:

Buyer shall be entitled a key and be entitled to access to show partners, lenders, inspectors, and/or contractors prior to closing. Buyer may place an appropriate sign on the property prior to closing for prospective tenants and/or assigns.

Key Points to Remember

- Understand the basic principles of contract law.
- Put up as little earnest money as possible.
- Learn how to draft a contract based on the standard form.

CHAPTER 7

Finding the Money to Buy the Properties

As a property flipper, your ideal transaction would be to assign your contract or close simultaneously with a buyer so that you have no cash out of pocket. If you have no money and cannot find a buyer before your closing date, you would lose your investment; i.e., your earnest money. Furthermore, if you intended to sell the property retail, you would need funds to close, carry, and rehab the property.

Acquiring loans to purchase properties is less difficult than you may think. Many beginning investors are afraid to make offers because they are uncertain how they will obtain the money needed to purchase. Have faith; if you can negotiate a good enough deal, the money will surely find you!

GOOD CREDIT IS A PLUS, BUT NOT A NECESSITY

Good credit will increase your financing choices, but it is not a necessity for buying real estate. You should line up your financing options as soon as possible. This may involve using your own cash, a partner's cash, or a bank loan, or having another investor to whom you sell the property. As discussed in Chapter 1, you should always know your backdoor first.

Having fast access to cash means having the ability to close quickly. Often, motivated sellers will accept the lower of two offers because one buyer can close more quickly. Other sellers may accept a lower offer because one buyer's ability to obtain financing looked more solid. As you begin to juggle multiple deals or aspire to purchase properties to hold, your financing knowledge (or lack thereof) can determine how successful you will ultimately be.

USING YOUR OWN CASH

If you are in a market where junker houses sell for $10,000, you can certainly use all cash to buy properties. In New York City or the San Francisco Bay Area, where the junker properties often sell for more than $200,000, this may be a bit more difficult. Furthermore, it may not be an effective use of your money, for the ability to make deals will be limited to the amount of cash you have on hand. The sale of a house may be delayed for any number of reasons, which may mean lost opportunities. Rehab properties tend to take longer than originally expected, and often go over budget. You should not use all cash unless you have an unlimited supply or have a guaranteed out within a short time. Even if you have a lot of cash, resist the temptation to use it. Experienced investors often reveal that they make some of their worst decisions when they have a lot of cash on hand. Having very little cash forces you to think creatively; no matter how much cash you have, pretend you don't have it!

Exception to the All-Cash Rule

One minor exception to the all-cash rule is to use your IRA/ SEP money to fund your purchases. You can use this money to buy and sell real estate tax-free. If you do not have a self-directed IRA or SEP, contact Mid Ohio Securities <www.midoh.com>. ■

Use Your Cash to Bring in Business

As with any start-up business, your cash is best spent marketing and advertising. If you have available cash, use it to get the phone ringing with motivated sellers. You may lose a few deals for lack of cash for buying properties, but you will have more overall business (and you don't need to worry about disappointed customers, for this is rarely a repeat sale business!).

There is an unlimited supply of private money available for profitable deals. Of course, when you go outside for money, you must give up some of the profit. If you do not have enough cash, three options are available:

1. Borrow the money.
2. Bring in partners.
3. Have the seller finance the transaction.

BORROWING MONEY

Your financing needs will vary depending on the type of property you select and on how long you intend to keep the property. The focus of this book is on flipping properties, so we won't spend too much time on borrowing money the old-fashioned way. Whenever you borrow money, you increase your risk of loss, so get your feet wet by flipping a few deals before thinking about borrowing money.

Institutional Financing

If you have spotless credit and a substantial salary or other source of income, borrowing money from institutional lenders is easy. You can easily obtain low-interest-rate loans for investment properties with a 20 percent down payment or more. Some loan programs will permit you to put as little as 10 percent down, but these programs are very stringent.

If you intend to sell the property to a retail buyer within a few months, you should not be concerned about the interest rate, but rather about the cost of the loan. Lenders charge points, which is a fancy name for profit. Each point is a percent of the loan; for example, on a $100,000 loan, 1.5 points amount to $1,500. This fee is paid when you originate the loan. Beware of other hidden charges, such as origination fees, loan review, underwriting, and other garbage fees—they all mean cash out of your pocket at closing. Also, make sure that your loan does not have a prepayment penalty, which is another fee that must be paid when you pay off the loan early.

Once you are more experienced at estimating repair costs, fixing properties, and marketing them for resale, you may consider using institutional lending, for it is a reliable way to purchase properties.

Friends and Relatives

Surely, friends and relatives are obvious choices for borrowing money, but they may be as skeptical as an institutional lender if you have no experience in real estate. They may also try to boss you around and nag you about repaying the money you borrowed. Do yourself a favor and wait until you have more experience before approaching friends and relatives. Once they see you making money, they will come to you!

Private Money

Look in the Real Estate Classified section of your newspaper under Money to Loan. You will find dozens of advertisements for private moneylenders. The rates they charge are almost criminal—as much as 18 percent with ten points in fees! While these rates may seem absurd, keep in mind that it is the availability of the money that counts more than the cost of borrowing it.

Many of these lenders (called hard-money lenders) will lend without proof of income or a credit report. Their loan criteria are based on the value of the property. They will usually loan anywhere from 50 percent to 70 percent of the appraised value of the property. If you have negotiated a price that is 80 percent of the market value of the property, you don't need to come up with a lot of cash. Institutional lenders, on the other hand, penalize you for negotiating a good deal by basing the loan on the appraised value or the purchase price, whichever is less.

Example: Property with a market value (after repairs) of $100,000. The property will appraise in its present condition for $90,000. You negotiate a purchase price of $70,000. A hard-money lender may lend you 70 percent of its appraised value, which is $63,000. This means you need only $7,000 of your own cash to close (plus, of course, closing costs). An institutional lender will lend you up to 90 percent of the purchase price, which is $63,000. The interest rate is lower on the institutional loan, but it is much harder to qualify for.

Credit Cards and Credit Lines

You may already have more available credit than you realize. Credit cards and other existing revolving debt accounts can be quite useful in real estate investing. Most major credit cards allow you to take cash advances or write checks to borrow on the account. The transaction fees and interest rates are fairly high, but you can access this money on 24 hours' notice. Also, you won't have to pay loan costs are normally associated with a real estate transaction, such as title insurance, appraisals, pest inspections, surveys, etc. Often, you will be better off paying 18 percent interest or more on a credit line for six months than paying 9 percent interest on an institutional loan, which has up-front costs that would take you years to recoup.

Promotional interest rates are often available on your credit cards, but again, beware. These rates often skyrocket after several months. Chances are, if you have a good credit history, you will be able to raise your credit limits on your existing cards. Creditors do not need to know you will be using your credit cards for the business of investing. Ironically, these creditors would rather see you using credit-line increases for typical consumer purchases that depreciate in value and produce no income.

High interest debt must be approached cautiously, and your personality type may not embrace the idea of tens of thousands of dollars in revolving debt. However, avoiding mortgages can be helpful in saving time and often money for short-term borrowing, so keep credit cards in mind. You can also benefit by using department-store cards with no cash advance features. These cards are available through all the major lumberyards, hardware-store chains, and home-improvement stores and they will allow you to finance your materials costs that can involve many thousands of dollars. The interest you pay for the use of this money is deductible, so be careful to separate your business from your personal credit card use.

BRING IN PARTNERS

Bringing in partners is a good way to start if you are flat broke and lack experience. But choose your partners carefully. Don't select a partner who contributes the same thing you do; e.g., enthusiasm and no money. Don't pick a partner because he is your friend or you think it would be fun to be in business together. Choose a partner with money and experience in real estate who can fund a deal that you have negotiated. If you are really green, you should consider flipping the property to him for a quick buck. If you want to see the process through to the retail buyer (and want to make more profit), then using a partner with money and experience is a worthwhile venture.

How to Split the Profits

Every deal will be different, but start the negotiating with a 50-50 profit split. The partner putting up the money and doing the work may insist on more of the profit, for he may be doing more of the work, such as supervising the workers. Based on the estimated sales price, purchase costs, and repairs, you can make a reasonable estimate of the total net profit. If your percentage is not sufficient, consider flipping the property to the investor and moving on to the next deal.

Joint Venture Agreement

If you choose to take on a partner for a deal, this is called a joint venture. A joint venture is a limited-purpose partnership. You should have a written joint agreement with your partner that spells out, among other things, the duties of each party and the manner in which money is contributed (see sample joint venture agreement in Appendix C). For a long-term partnership arrangement, consider a corporation or limited liability company (see Chapter 10).

HAVE THE SELLER FINANCE THE PURCHASE

Having the seller finance the sale, even in part, is the best way to purchase a property. It does not require bank qualification, credit, personal liability, or garbage fees. If you don't have loan costs involved in the transaction, you can afford to pay the seller a higher price.

Owner-Carry Sale

As discussed in Chapter 2, an owner-carry transaction or installment sale occurs whenever the seller takes less than all cash for the purchase price. Keep in mind that all cash does not necessarily mean that you paid cash out of your pocket; it also means borrowed money. The less of the purchase price you have to pay, the better the deal becomes, even if you flip the property to another investor. The ideal scenario would be if the seller owned the property free and clear, and took a small cash down payment and a note for the balance of the purchase price. In the real world, this event rarely happens.

Buying "Subject to" the Existing Loan

As discussed in Chapter 2, when you transfer title to a property without paying off or assuming the existing loan, you are taking the property subject to the existing loan. In most cases, the mortgage or deed of trust securing the existing loan contains a due-on-sale restriction, allowing the lender to call the balance owed immediately due and payable. Because you will have title only for a short period of time, this issue is, at least to you, wholly irrelevant. You will have sold the property long before the lender discovers the transfer and decides to initiate foreclosure proceedings.

When Taking Subject To:

- Get a power of attorney so you can deal with his lender for payoff information, or in case you did something wrong with the execution of the original deed and cannot get in touch with the seller.
- Get the seller's payment booklet or last monthly statement and send in a change-of-address form.
- Have the seller sign a due-on-sale acknowledgment (see Appendix C) about the fact that you are not assuming his loan and it will remain on his credit report until you pay it off.

If you can buy a property subject to the existing loan, you will save thousands of dollars in loan origination costs, closing costs, and other garbage fees. Ideally, you could find out what the seller wants to net in cash from the transactions, then pay him that cash and have him deed you the property subject to the existing loan. Of course, the total purchase price would have to be low enough for you to make a profit. If the property is in foreclosure, it will not be difficult for you to convince the seller to deed you the property in exchange for some cash and your promise to make up the back payments on his loan and continue making payments.

The problem, however, is convincing a seller who is current on his payments that you will make payments after he deeds the property to you. Remember that once he deeds you the property, he has no recourse against the property if you fail to make the payments on his loan. His credit will be adversely affected if you fail to make timely payments on his loan. So the issue becomes, "How do you convince the seller to deed you the property?"

The real issue for the seller is, "How do I know you'll make the payments?" The seller wants finality; he wants his loan paid off completely and removed from his credit report.

You could start by simply telling him your intentions, which are that you are going to fix up the property and sell it to a retail buyer, at which time you will pay off his loan. In the meantime, you will continue making his payments. If this is not good enough, simply insert a clause into the purchase contract that states as follows:

> Purchaser agrees to satisfy seller's loan with _____ bank loan # _____ on or before _____, 2001, and further agrees to make timely monthly payments required by said lender, including tax and insurance escrows as they become due. This clause shall survive closing of the title.

The payoff date should be out at least six months, preferably one year. Of course, the seller's legal recourse is to sue if you don't perform given that he has no recourse against the property. If he is savvy enough (or concerned enough) to understand his legal position, offer him a second mortgage on the property. This mortgage is for a nominal amount, such as $10, but states that your failure to make payment on his underlying mortgage places you in default of the second mortgage. Thus, if you failed to make payments, he would have the right to foreclose against the property to get the title back.

Another way to make him feel more secure would be to set up a third-party escrow with a collection company. This company would collect payments from you each month, send them to the lender, and send a copy to the seller. A more practical way to accomplish the same task would be to set up a bank account with a direct deposit to the lender. The bank would send the seller duplicate copies of the bank statements each month. Several automated services on the Internet also will do this for you, such as <www.paytrust.com>. Wells Fargo Bank also has online automated banking services.

Another Option: Installment Land Contract

If the seller will not hand over the deed, consider using an installment land contract (see Chapter 2). This creates a wraparound transaction (see Figure 7.1) in which you make payments to the seller and he makes them to the bank. This is similar to the way banks handle car loans; they hold title as security for payment until the loan is paid off. For tax purposes, an installment land contract is a sale, but it puts the buyer in a weaker or legal position. If the seller refuses to convey title when you tender the balance of the purchase price, you must sue him in court. Investors don't make money in court, lawyers do. Make sure you approach a land contract with caution, having an experienced attorney review the documents. Also, consider taking a home study course such as "Alternative Real Estate Financing," which provides all the forms and

FIGURE 7.1
Installment Land Contract

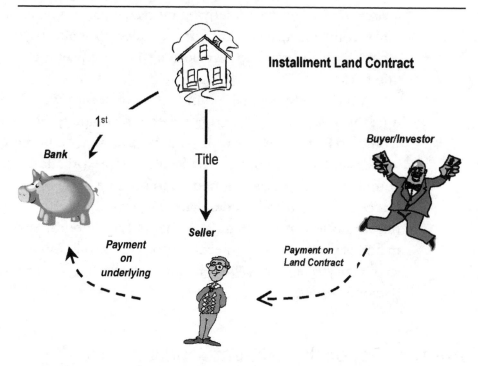

instructions on how to handle installment land contracts the right way. Call Legalwiz Publications tollfree at 800-655-3632 or visit <www.legalwiz.com>.

Key Points to Remember

- Line up your financing options before making an offer.
- Be careful about using partners.
- Learn how to take subject to existing loans.

CHAPTER 8

The Closing Process

A closing is nothing more than a delivery of cash by the buyer and an execution and delivery of the deed from the seller. However, many significant events occur between contract and closing. Usually, the real estate agents, attorneys, and title company representatives handle most of these tasks. Regardless of whether you do your own closing or use a title or escrow company, you should be familiar with these tasks.

THE PROPERTY INSPECTION

If the contract calls for an inspection by the buyer, this should happen immediately, especially if there is a deadline. If the buyer is not experienced, she should consider employing a contractor or a professional house inspector. For about $150 in most areas, a house inspection service will prepare a detailed report and a list

list to her advantage to negotiate a lower price. The buyer can also use the inspection clause to kill a deal that turned out to be a bad choice on her part. If the seller will not agree to make the necessary repairs or adjustments to the price, the buyer can cancel the contract and receive her earnest money back.

If you are planning to flip the property to another investor, you should bring interested investors with you when you conduct the inspection. Furthermore, you should have a provision in the contract (see Chapter 6) that allows you access to the property at reasonable times so you can show it to prospective buyers.

TITLE AND TITLE SEARCHES

A real estate contract usually requires that title to the property be marketable, that is, it must have no serious defects that would prevent it from being mortgaged or sold at a later time. A buyer also wants marketable title so that she feels secure that no one is going to sue her or claim an interest in the property.

A title search is an inspection of the public records that relate to the property. While a deed is evidence of ownership, it is not the complete picture; title is proof of ownership. For example, a deed held by a seller on a land contract is not complete ownership, for the land contract buyer has equitable title. Having equitable title does not mean the buyer's name is on the deed recorded in public records; the equitable owner has the right to receive the legal title (deed) when the balance owed on the land contract has been paid.

The Recording Index

Virtually every county in the United States has a place where records of title are publicly recorded. In most cases, it will be the office of the county clerk and recorder or the county courthouse. All records are copied onto computers or microfiche, then recorded in large ledger books. Most areas of the country have begun using computers to index documents.

Understanding the Terminology

The giver of any interest in real estate is called the grantor; the receiver of the interest is the grantee. On some documents, the grantor and grantee are called by other terms. For example, on a deed, the grantor is also the seller, the grantee the buyer. On a mortgage, the grantor is also called the mortgagor and borrower; the lender is the grantee and mortgagee. On a deed of trust, the grantor is sometimes called the trustor; the lender is the beneficiary. Regardless of the name, everything is indexed in county records as grantor/grantee. ■

The most common indexing system is by grantor and grantee. All documents conveying property interests are recorded by the grantor's last name in the grantor index. The same transaction is cross-indexed by the grantee's last name in the grantee index.

Conducting a Title Search

A title search is important because it will determine if title is good and marketable. To determine if title is good, you must follow the chain of title as it changed hands over the years. A break in the chain of title will create a gap, which can result in confusion over ownership. Theoretically, the chain of title must be followed back to the Native Americans, or at least as far as the ascertainable records will show. In practice, the chain of title is only searched back about 50 years.

A title search can be conducted with a title company for a fee or, as an educational exercise, you can do it yourself. If you hang around the county recorder's office, you can usually find a title company employee who would be happy to assist you for a few bucks. In addition to the chain of title, make certain that you also check for unpaid property taxes, assessments, homeowners association dues, water and sewer charges, restrictive covenants, judgments, bankruptcy petitions, and other possible liens that are not recorded in county land records. If this process sounds confusing, don't worry, it is! Be smart and pay for a title search the first few times you buy property. Do not, however, waste time checking title until you have a signed contract with the seller.

Saving Money on Title Insurance

Title insurance, like any insurance, defends and pays claims against the insured. In the case of real estate, the buyer is the insured. Thus, if anyone makes a claim against the buyer's interest in the property, the title insurance company must defend that claim and pay any damages suffered by the buyer because of the claim. Typical claims involve liens not discovered until after the closing, forgeries or errors from previous deeds in the chain of title, and easements or rights-of-way that were not known. While purchasing title insurance may seem entirely reasonable, it can, in some cases, be a waste of money.

If you have little money invested in a transaction, you have very little to lose. For example, if you give a seller $1,000 to deed you the property, what is the limit of your loss? The answer is obviously $1,000, so why would you pay $700 for a title insurance policy if there was no apparent risk of a title problem? As you become more experienced, you will see that purchasing a title insurance policy is not always necessary, particularly when you intend to flip the property to another investor for a quick buck. Undoubtedly, that investor will buy title insurance if she intends to resell the property after putting up several thousand dollars for repairs.

Let's be clear, however, that we do not recommend you buy and sell property as a beginner without checking title or buying title insurance. This technique must be learned through experience and knowledge. Always do things the conservative and safe way when starting out. If the deal is a little thin on profit, simply assign your contract, in which case title insurance won't be necessary.

Ask for a Reissue Rate: If you do purchase a title policy when doing a double closing, ask for a discounted rate. If the property was sold or refinanced within the past few years, most title insurance companies will offer a discounted rate, for their risk is lower. Make sure you *ask*—they won't always offer it up front!

Ask for a "Hold Open" Policy: If you intend to resell the property when you buy, whether in a double closing or within six months, ask for a "hold-open" policy. This type of policy costs an extra 10 percent to 20 percent up front and will cover title upon resale within 12 months (some companies will cover you up to 24 months). The policy may be called by another name in some states, so ask your title insurance representative. Because the seller usually pays for title insurance, your cost will be 10 to 20 percent of a full policy.

EXISTING MORTGAGES AND LIENS

If you are paying off existing mortgages or other liens, you must contact the holders of these mortgages or liens for payoff information. Make certain you verify that the holder of the lien or mortgage has an original document that can be delivered to you upon satisfaction of the underlying obligation. You should get original promissory notes back marked "paid in full." If you are dealing with private mortgage or lien holders, remember to ask for a discount!

THE CLOSING

A title insurance company usually handles the closing. Title companies perform three services: searching title, selling title insurance, and performing the closing. The closing or escrow closing is the ceremony of executing and delivering deeds, signing loan documents, collecting and disbursing funds, and recording documents. In some states, attorneys do the title search and the closing. In other states, a separate escrow company performs the closing services. Either way, make certain that the closing agent, attorney, or company is familiar with the double closing process. If you are told it is illegal, unethical, or not possible, call someone else. Double closings are transacted in every state, every day of the week.

The formal closing usually involves sitting at a big oak table at a title company or attorney's office. In some states, such as California, closings are done in escrow (see Chapter 2). Both buyer and seller, not necessarily at the same time, sign documents that are held by the closing agent. When the buyer's lender approves the transaction, it funds the loan and the transaction is complete when the funds are distributed and the documents are recorded.

In most states, closings are table funded, that is, the funds are distributed at the table when all the parties finish signing documents. In this case, both the seller and the buyer are present. If you are doing a double closing, you are acting as both buyer and seller. A double closing is really two separate transactions and can be handled in two phases if you do not want your retail investor to meet the seller you purchased from. Obviously, you cannot give the seller funds until your investor gives you funds. Thus, one of the two transactions must be closed in escrow until the other is complete. Oftentimes, this escrow may last an hour. The bottom line is that if your investor does not deliver funds and sign all the closing documents, you cannot close with your seller.

Key Points to Remember

- Have the property inspected carefully.
- Make sure the title is marketable.
- Ask for the appropriate discount for title insurance.

CHAPTER 9

Rehab Properties: The Big Bucks!

The investor who fixes up the property and sells it to an owner-occupant earns the lion's share of profit on each deal. Because he must invest the most cash, labor, and time, the retailer also takes the largest risk. This chapter discusses how to estimate repairs, what items to fix, and how to hire the necessary help to get the job done.

IS THE REHAB BUSINESS FOR YOU?

Before you enter the rehab business, you must decide if it is for you. Some people like being hands-on. Other people are all thumbs and have no business doing fix-up work. Determine whether getting involved in the rehab business is the most effective use of your time. If you can hire a contractor to handle your projects, you will have more free time to find and negotiate deals.

You may decide to take on a partner who will handle the rehab business while you take care of the financing and the paperwork. Whichever way you choose, always be involved in managing the process or it will get away from you. You cannot afford to fall behind your schedule, or to go over budget.

HOW MUCH REHAB KNOWLEDGE IS NECESSARY?

Most of your best real estate deals will involve properties that are in desperate need of repairs. Rarely will you find a bargain property that is in perfect condition. Thus, you need to have a basic idea of how much time and money it will take to bring the property up to salable condition, meaning that it is clean, new, and attractive.

Many real estate investors have become wealthy without having any knowledge of construction. However, an even greater number of investors have lost money because they did not have enough construction experience. Whether you intend to fix up properties yourself or flip them to other investors, start with a basic rehab job that requires cleanup, carpet, paint, and landscaping. These items are cosmetic and do not require any special knowledge, just labor and the cost of materials. If you ever tackle bigger projects such as additions or completely gutting a house, the local building department will usually insist that you also update wiring or mechanical systems. Smaller jobs generally can be done without a permit.

Tip on Work Permits

Ask other contractors about what you can do without a permit before asking the city building department. The city code may require you to get a permit to change a lightbulb, but the local contractors know what repairs you can get away with without a permit. ▪

As stated earlier, you should utilize the services of an experienced inspection service to thoroughly evaluate the property prior to purchase. Only buy properties when you feel comfortable with the level of repairs needed. Just about anyone can remove trash, clean, paint, and landscape a run-down property. Over time, you can tackle more difficult projects. Sweat equity (doing it yourself) can earn you extra money on every deal if you have the time available. The more time you spend supervising the project, the more you will learn about the process and the faster it will get done. If you handle a more complex project, make sure you have experienced help available and that you carefully budget all labor and materials costs.

ESTIMATING REPAIRS

Both beginning and experienced investors habitually underestimate the time and expense needed to complete a renovation. Always estimate repairs conservatively, considering the worst-case scenario. Start with the outside and work through the inside, room by room, step by step. Use the checklist in Figure 9.1 to come up with an estimate of repairs, and then add at least a 10 percent margin for error. If you sell the property retail, any overestimate will become an extra bonus. If you are a dealer and underestimate the repairs, the experienced retailer will spot this and will not be enthusiastic about doing business with you in the future.

FIGURE 9.1
Checklist of Repair/Replacement Items

	Cost of Materials	Labor Hours	Totals
Kitchen			
❏ Stainless-steel sink with faucet	100	3.5	
❏ Ceiling light (use same throughout the house)	20	.5	
❏ Countertop with backsplash (per 10 feet)	75	2	
❏ Cabinet knobs (for 25)	35	2	
❏ Basic electric range (basic model new)	300	2	
❏ Dishwasher (basic model new/nice model used)	250	3	
Bathrooms			
❏ Vanity with faucet	125	3.5	
❏ Toilet with seat	100	2	
❏ Towel bar set	25	.5	
❏ Tub surround kit (replaces worn tile)	100	3	
❏ Medicine cabinet	75	1	
❏ Light fixture	25	.5	
Master Bedroom			
❏ Closet doors (4-ft. unpainted)	65	3	
❏ Ceiling fan with light	65	2	
❏ Door (match existing style)	30	2	
❏ Doorknobs (brass set with locks)	15	.25	
Floor Coverings (professionally installed per sq. ft.)			
❏ Sheet vinyl	2	N/A	
❏ Tile (use 12″ × 12″ neutral colors)	5	N/A	
❏ Carpet (with pad)	2	N/A	
Other Interior Materials			
❏ Molding (preprimed per linear foot)	.50	.1	
❏ Interior eggshell paint (per 5 gallons)	.70	8	
Exterior Items			
❏ Exterior flat paint (per 5 gallons)	85	8	
❏ Exterior light fixture (brass)	25	.5	
❏ Basic single-pane window (installed)	100	N/A	
❏ Window screen	25	.5	
❏ Front door	150	3	
❏ Roof shingles (installed) 1,200 sq. foot ranch	2,100	N/A	
❏ Front porch stoop repair (including labor)	150	N/A	
❏ Seamless gutters (installed per linear foot)	3	N/A	
Landscape Projects			
❏ New sod (installed per sq. ft.)	.75	N/A	
❏ Juniper bush (3-ft. tall per bush)	40	.5	
❏ 6-ft. privacy fence (per linear ft., 8-ft. lengths)	10	N/A	
❏ Organic cedar mulch (delivered per cubic yard)	25	.1	

But I Don't Even Know How to Fix a Toilet!

If you never so much as picked up a hammer, a repair checklist may not mean much. One way you will become better at estimating costs is to learn how the work is done. We are not suggesting that you learn the physical skills necessary to do each job, but rather the overall process. Once you understand the mechanics of each part of the job, you will become confident estimating the repairs and negotiating with the contractors. The major home improvement chains, such as Home Depot, give free classes on everything from tiling kitchens to replacing windows. Books and videos on basic home improvement are also available from Home Depot, *Reader's Digest,* and *Time Life.* Gathering this information will give you a good idea of the time, materials, and cost of the needed repairs. It will also arm you with enough knowledge to know when a contractor is ripping you off!

Learn the Cost of Your Materials and Labor

Spend a few hours in home improvement stores such as Home Depot, noting the cost of various items you are likely to purchase for your projects. Remember to buy budget-oriented materials. Avoid special order items; buy closeouts or "scratch and dents" when possible.

Once you learn the cost of replacement items, you must learn how much labor will be involved in replacing or installing the items. If you possess basic handyman skills, you can do some of the work yourself, following the books and videos described earlier. Always assume, however, that you are going to hire out the labor when calculating repair costs.

Estimating Labor Costs

In general, most basic items will cost you 50¢ to $1 in labor to install each dollar of material. Thus, a $20 light should cost you $10 to $20 of labor to have it installed. This guideline does not necessarily apply to all items. Of course, a $200 light fixture will not cost you $100 to $200 in labor to install. The labor costs will also vary, depending on the caliber of labor you employ and the area of the country you live in. The costs will also vary according to unforeseen problems that often arise when re-placing certain items. ▪

There is no exact scientific formula for estimating repair costs on a rehab. The truth is, estimating repair costs is more of an art than a science. Like any art, it takes practice and experience to master. Our goal is to get you thinking and looking for things that may need repair or replacement so that you can come up with a rough estimate. Once you have a rough estimate, you can prepare an offer to the seller. If you are insecure about your assessment of the property, just reflect that in your offer. Unless the seller is a contractor, you will know more about the cost of doing the repairs than he will. Thus, he may think it will cost more than necessary to fix up the property and be willing to accept a lower price.

Get Bids from at Least Three Contractors

Whether you intend to do a job yourself or hire help, get three contractors to bid on the work. Spend some time with each one and ask a lot of questions. When you hear the same thing three times, you start to understand it a little better. If one contractor claims a particular project is difficult and expensive, then have him explain the specific issues to you. If another contractor says the job is simple, repeat what the first contractor said and listen for her response. Her answer will help you to determine if someone is fibbing or is more experienced. Usually, there are several ways to address a problem. As you gain experience, you will be able to quickly make sound decisions on how to approach each aspect of renovating a property. Aim for simple, fast, and cost-effective repairs.

WHAT SHOULD I FIX?

Many seminars teach investment students a cookie-cutter approach to rehabs. While you should be systematic in your approach to rehabs, please note that every property is different. Location and potential value, age, and the architectural style of a property will affect how you should approach the renovation. The condition of the property or the scope of the needed repairs will also affect the rehab process.

Determine How Nice Your House Should Be

Before your fix-up begins, assess the neighborhood, carefully determining the scope of your repairs. Try to be consistent with the neighborhood, but make your house just a little nicer. You can easily overdo it if you are not careful. Do not go overboard regarding quality of materials, time spent on minor details, or unimportant problems. Only do things that add value and salability to the house. It is common for beginners to spend time and money on unnecessary projects. As a result, these beginners must ask premium prices for their properties, wasting time and money waiting for their houses to sell. A rule of thumb is to only tackle projects that will add twice the cost of their renovations to the home's value.

You never want the most expensive house in a neighborhood, just the cleanest. The standard items should be consistent with the neighborhood. For example, window air conditioners may be the norm in one neighborhood, but central air may be standard in another. Don't install central air-conditioning in a window-unit neighborhood. Items such as new windows, sprinkler systems, security alarms, and storm doors are not usually worth the cost and effort to install. On the other hand, *do* be generous on the cheap items—ceiling fans, doorknobs, switch plates, toilet seats, faucets, trim, bushes, and other cosmetic items.

Locate Help for the Repairs

Once you plan the individual projects for a rehab, you must decide which projects you will delegate. Balance out your need to learn about construction with your available time. Of course, you will have to pay someone else to complete the projects that are beyond your abilities.

Where to Find Help: Over time you will develop a network of helpers. As you get to know other real estate professionals, you will be able to get referrals for most of the contractors you will need. Until then, you can find handyman types to fill most of your needs through local newspapers under the Services Offered category. Visit local construction sites to find skilled tradesmen such as roofers, framers, and ceramic tile installers. Often these people are willing to moonlight, and will save you money compared with using large companies. Sometimes you will have to refer to your Yellow Pages for specialized help.

How Much to Pay: Treat every aspect of a renovation as a challenge to get the maximum value for the money spent. Generally, you can save money on labor by paying cash. There are tax implications regarding cash payments, contractor labor, and employee issues, so consult a tax advisor before you get in over your head. You should be able to find labor for about $12 an hour, maybe less. You will need skilled contractors for some jobs. Expect to pay these people closer to $25 per hour. Learning a little about each of the various building trades such as plumbing, electrical, heating, framing, and finish carpentry will enable you to critique the work of your subcontractors. Eventually, you will undertake jobs that require the services of licensed tradesmen. Expect to pay a little extra for licensed individuals. Here are a few tips on hiring:

- Negotiate with contractors, suppliers, and other service providers.
- Go with smaller companies to earn discounts and develop loyalty.
- Do a reasonable amount of homework on your new associates.
- Always be on the lookout for affordable, yet reliable contractors.
- Pay for the larger jobs on a bid basis.
- Ask contractors to show proof of disability and liability insurance.

Insurance

Always carry fire and hazard insurance on any properties you purchase. In addition, you should carry liability insurance once you begin hiring helpers. Most run-down properties qualify for a landlord-type policy, and larger projects can be covered by a builder's risk policy. The builder's risk policy will be more costly, so use it as a last resort. ▪

Get It in Writing: As mentioned earlier, outsource bids for your larger projects. You can reduce risk and save money by paying contractors for the complete job. Once you know your contractors, and can calculate the time involved in each task, you can pay based on time and materials. Create a written agreement with each contractor you hire (see the sample Independent Contractor Agreement in Appendix C). Spell out exactly what he is to do, how long it will take, and how he will be paid. Do not pay contractors in advance, and do create monetary incentives for staying on schedule. And keep a copy of the contractor's proof of insurance on file.

REPAIRS ON THE INSIDE

We will walk you through the rehab process on a typical two-bedroom, one-bath project house. We will assume the house has working mechanical systems and is structurally sound. We will also assume that you are no Bob Vila, but that you can handle basic tasks such as replacing a bathroom vanity and installing a medicine cabinet. If you cannot or choose not to do these things yourself, then factor in the cost of a handyman to help.

Why Start with the Inside?

Some retailers recommend that you start with the outside of the house to attract potential buyers as early as possible. We disagree.

You never want to draw undo attention to the fact that you are doing extensive repairs. Working on the inside first will allow you to maintain a relatively low profile. If a nosy neighbor or potential buyer stops by, tell him to come back in a couple weeks for a tour. By the time he returns you will have cleaned up the debris, animal odors, and unsafe conditions left by previous inhabitants. Most potential buyers lack the imagination to preview a property in the early stages of renovation. Other than for serious investors, it simply does not pay to show the property too early. Once the inside is clean and viewable, start fixing the outside and put up a For Sale sign.

The Kitchen

Married couples buy most houses, and the first place house hunters want to see is the kitchen. The kitchen should be relatively modern, bright, and, like the rest of the house, sparkling clean. Always use semigloss paint in the kitchen, as well as in the bathrooms. Cabinets can be wiped with lemon oil–based products to bring back their shine. If they are dull or dark brown, paint them with a high-gloss white. Use an oil-based primer and replace all knobs and hinges with new ones.

Replace any appliances that are not black, white, or ivory. If it doesn't look clean and nice, replace it. You can buy a new stove or dishwasher for a few hundred dollars at a retail chain store, such as Best Buy. For the same price, you can buy a slightly better model at a local secondhand appliance store. Many of the used-appliance stores will install the appliance and haul away the old one for a nominal amount.

Throw Out an Ugly Fridge

Unless the fridge is very nice and clean, throw it out. Most houses today are sold without a fridge. An ugly fridge looks worse than no fridge, especially if it is very large and the kitchen is relatively small. ▪

A fancy, modern faucet looks great in the kitchen. The best faucets can cost as much as $300, so don't get carried away. You can usually find a very nice faucet on sale for under $75. Sinks and countertops should not date the kitchen, either. If they don't complement the kitchen, replace the counters with inexpensive units with a built-in backsplash. You may need an experienced handyman to help you install the counters.

Replace any dated light fixtures with new ones. You will need professional assistance on electrical projects at first. Take time to learn about electrical systems and always respect the potential dangers! We suggest replacing the kitchen and bathroom electrical outlets with ground fault circuit interrupter units (GFCIs). These GFCIs help prevent electrical shocks and are required by code in wet areas of new construction, including kitchens, bathrooms, garages, and basements.

In other areas of the house, replace all the switch plates. This improvement is often overlooked. Most rehabbers paint a unit and leave the old, ugly switch plates. Even worse, some even paint over them. New switch plates cost about 50¢ each. You can replace an entire house with new switch plates for about $20. For the foyer, living room, and other showcase areas, indulge and buy nice brass plates. They run about $5 each—not much for the added class.

The Bathrooms

The bathroom is another important area. You may not be able to enlarge it, but make sure it is modern and bright, and not musty. Use vinegar and lime/rust removal products to clean up porcelain fixtures. If the tub is in poor condition, or is not white, then you can pay to have it refinished. The cost will be several hundred dollars, but refinishing a tub is simpler than replacing it. A tile surround in the tub area can usually be repaired and regrouted; however plastic surrounds in poor condition should be replaced. Remove the old shower curtain (in addition to any outdated window coverings in the house). The toilet and seat should be replaced if they cannot be cleaned to like-new condition. In addition, the sink and vanity should be replaced if they are dated or damaged. Choose a new unit with a one-piece cultured marble top in a standard size.

Paint the bathrooms using a semigloss paint. White is a safe choice, but pale yellow, blue, or green are common in modern houses. A matching wallpaper border along the ceiling is a nice touch. If the bathroom has old wallpaper and it is properly hung and not textured, you can paint right over it, using a primer first. If the paper is textured or if it is peeling, you must remove it.

The Master Bedroom and Other Living Space

Ceiling fans are inexpensive upgrades for the bedrooms and living room, unless the house has low ceilings. Decide where you will place fans before painting, and make sure the electrical junction boxes in the ceiling are designed for the weight of a fan. Replace any old or dull light fixtures with new ones.

Check that doors work properly and replace ugly or broken doorknobs. Mirrored sliding closet doors make a room look larger. Verify the height of the existing opening before purchasing them because you cannot shorten mirrored doors. It is especially important that the front door works properly; otherwise you will frustrate a potential buyer before he makes it inside the property.

Replace any damaged or old brown doors with new white ones. If you are replacing all the doors, consider six-panel, hollow-core doors. They cost just a few bucks more than standard hollow-core doors, but they look very stylish. Doors with a natural or stain finish can be wiped down with lemon oil or a light stain to bring them back to life.

In addition to changing doors, change the knobs. An old doorknob, especially with crusted paint on it, looks drab. For about $10, you can replace it with a new brass-finished model. Replace bathroom and bedroom door handles with the fancy "S" handles, which cost about $20 per set.

Flooring

Flooring is a major expense in most renovations. Hardwood floors are often hidden under outdated carpets. The hardwood is worth restoring in most cases. Refinishing floors is not a do-it-yourself project. The cost of equipment rentals and the disappointing results that follow are reasons not to tackle the project. Professionals will repair, sand, and refinish the floor for as low as $2 per square foot. Flooring for the kitchen, bath, entryway, and laundry room should be vinyl or tile. Tile floors and tub surrounds are nice upgrades if you can learn to lay tile or find someone else to do it inexpensively.

Install new carpet throughout the remainder of the house. Carpet can be used in a bathroom to save money if the bathroom floor is in poor condition. Light beige is a safe bet for carpet color. You can find nice carpeting at bargain warehouses; ask for over-runs, which are rolls left over from larger jobs. Many discount carpet stores will discount the price of the carpet if you use their carpet installers.

Choose at least one grade above the FHA minimum standard and use a closed cell rebound-type pad. If you can spare the expense, a Berber carpet looks dynamite. Make sure that your installers are experienced with Berber, for it is not easy to install. The money saved by going with a low-end carpet may be lost many times over if the property does not show well.

Mechanical Systems

Every property you sell should be in top-notch mechanical condition. Some type of central heating system is mandatory. Quality workmanship shows, and even first-time buyers will recognize shoddy workmanship. The problems your buyers miss will probably be noticed if they hire a professional home inspector, and these problems may jeopardize the sale. Other well-hidden shortcuts could eventually lead to lawsuits, fires, or other tragedies. Fortunately, you will be paid back through personal and financial satisfaction by repairing it properly the first time. It is your responsibility to deliver a safe and sound home.

Carefully evaluate the furnace or other heating system and water heater. If you are uncertain, get a professional opinion or two. It is usually much easier to replace these devices before the property is in its salable condition.

Air-conditioning may be a worthwhile improvement in some parts of the country, depending on the neighborhood. If most homes in the neighborhood have central air, then so should your house. Window-type air-conditioning units are worth considering, but don't place these eyesores where they are visible from the street.

Safety Items

Always include at least two operable battery-powered smoke detectors. The National Electric Code calls for hard-wired interconnected smoke detectors with battery backups. However, the difficulty of installation may only warrant installation if other electrical improvements are made.

The property should also have securely locking exterior doors. Dead-bolt locks should allow the occupant to open the latch from inside the premises without a key (because of fire liability issues). Other items that buyers expect are window screens, a decent roof, and adequate insulation. Each bedroom will need a closet and a safe egress window. Nonconforming bedrooms may hurt the property's appraisal value, so try to provide at least two conforming bedrooms.

REPAIRS ON THE OUTSIDE

Any property with curb appeal is much easier to sell than an otherwise similar property that lags behind in exterior aesthetics. The exterior items you will be looking for are the paint, entryway, landscaping, roof, windows, gutters and downspouts, mailbox, and the neighborhood.

Paint

Paint goes a long, long way. The home should be an attractive neutral color with a fresh coat of paint. Light colors tend to make a house look larger. Warm shades of tan or gray are easier to keep clean than white is. Match colors to the roof and any stone or brickwork. Trim can be painted a separate color to accent architectural highlights, or can be left the same color as the body of the house. Accent the house with basic blues, beiges, and greens. Stay away from wild colors, such as purple, red, pink, and black. Visit model homes in a new subdivision to get an idea about colors. If the exterior of the house is a nice cedar shingle or vinyl, rent a pressure washer to clean it up rather than paint it.

Entryway

You only get one chance to make a first impression. A cheap front door makes a house look cheap. An old front door makes a house look old. If the front door is worn or very basic, spend $150 for a nice, new door. Paint it a bold burgundy or hunter green, using a semigloss enamel.

The entryway should be well lit with an attractive porch light. Many older homes have unattractive aluminum storm doors that you should discard or leave in the garage or basement for future owners. Add clearly visible house numbers and a decorative trim around the front door. Remove antennas or other unnecessary items that are visible from the street.

If the front stoop has enough cracks to make it unsightly or dangerous, you need to fix it. A wooden porch is fairly easy to repair. Use treated pressurized lumber and apply stain-and-weather treatment. It does not take specialized skills to fix a stoop, so any good handyman should be able to do it in an afternoon. A small concrete stoop can be repaired with a mixable concrete such as Quickcrete.

Landscaping

Landscaping should highlight the house without overpowering it. Prune bushes to thin out new growth, and cut trees that are too close to the house. The front should be nice and green. As a last resort the lawn can be resodded, but try to salvage it before starting over. Even a weed-infested lawn can look presentable if it is well watered and cut down low. Products such as Revive will bring the green back to most lawns, but will last only a few weeks.

Organic mulch will cover many faults in a yard. Mulch is a natural-looking substitute for grass and flower beds. Use it to create beds and borders around the house's foundation, and to cover weed-infested areas. Utilize bricks or inexpensive landscape timbers to make interesting beds and borders. Use mulch instead of gravel, for it costs less and is easier to work with. Gravel is also harder to remove if a buyer wants to do something different in an area.

Every home should have some plants and trees. If the front yard lacks greenery, plant a few inexpensive shrubs across the front of the house. Old, overgrown shrubs should be removed or trimmed back to a manageable size. Geraniums or other annuals add color during the warmer months. Use your imagination and you will be surprised how much a little effort will improve the outside of a property.

Roof

A roof is often overlooked by beginners and can be very expensive to replace. The most common type of shingles are made from asphalt. Check for buckled, cracked, or worn shingles. Use a ladder to get on the roof and take a closer look. If the roof looks good from the street, you may get away with replacing only a few shingles, which is fairly easy (but sometimes dangerous, if the roof is steep).

Check to see how many layers of shingles have been applied to the roof. In most areas of the country, three layers of shingle is the maximum amount that is acceptable. If there are three layers or more and the roof looks bad, one or more layers must be scraped off, and a new layer must be applied. This job should be left to the professionals, but shop around for a good price. Keep in mind that when the property is sold retail, the roof may have to conform with higher standards if the buyer applies for an FHA or a VA loan.

A basic 1,200-square-foot ranch house should cost you about $1,800 to reshingle. If the wood sheathing underneath is rotted, you will need to scrape off all of the layers of shingles and replace the underlayment, which could cost thousands more. Remember that a wood shake roof is much more expensive to replace than an asphalt shingle roof.

Windows

Sandpaper and soap can be used on old windows to get them working again. Window replacement, especially on older houses, is not a job for the beginning rehabber. When replacing any broken window panes and screens, hire a professional to do it!

If you have ugly aluminum-framed windows, consider adding wooden shutters on the outside. They come preprimed at most hardware retailers and are easy to install. Paint them an offset color from the outside of the house. If the house is dark, for example, paint the shutters white. If the house is light, paint them green, blue, or another contrasting color.

Gutters and Downspouts

A missing section of gutter or downspout can be purchased at a hardware store and installed rather quickly. If all the gutters are bad, consider hiring a professional to install seamless gutters (about $3/linear foot installed); they look much better than sectioned gutters. If it appears that the house hasn't had gutters in years and there is no drainage problem, don't bother installing gutters.

Mailbox

Everyone on the block has the same black mailbox. Stand out. Be bold! Spend about $30 for a nice mailbox. For another $50, you can buy a nice wooden post for it. People notice and appreciate these things.

Improve the Neighborhood

Sometimes the best thing you can do to improve a property's curb appeal is to improve the neighborhood. An ugly house next door to your shiny jewel will frighten away many potential buyers. If the house next door looks like a junkyard, then offer to clean it up. Explain that you will be hauling trash anyway and would be glad to take a little extra. Be diplomatic in your approach when approaching neighbors, for they may be offended or even become belligerent. You can also repair fences, landscape, or paint for adjacent property owners at a reduced cost.

PLANNING THE RENOVATION PROCESS

A vacant house will not make you any money, so do not underestimate the importance of completing the renovation quickly. Plan for the renovation process before the closing day. Schedule material deliveries so that you can begin work immediately after the purchase. Be prepared to cancel or postpone deliveries and subcontractors if the property does not close on time. Be sure the electric power, gas, and water will be working. It is important to maintain flexibility, which is another reason to minimize the use of special-order items for the property.

Locate Shutoffs

Locate the main electric panel and the gas and water shutoffs prior to starting work. Also locate the city water shutoff near the street. While you frantically try to stop the water flow from a broken pipe in an emergency and the water valve in the house breaks, you don't want to flood the house! ■

Start with Rubbish Removal

Plan on removing trash, unwanted carpets, and plumbing fixtures and starting any other demolition on the first workday. Be careful of hidden wiring and gas pipes, and do not tear out walls or other potentially structural items unless you are experienced! We have seen many circumstances where overzealous people have removed load-bearing walls and otherwise compromised a house's structural integrity.

As discussed, maintain a low profile during the renovation. Always schedule a trash-hauling service or rent a roll-off trash container for the beginning of the project. If you think you will have major trash removal later in the project, then place the trash in an inconspicuous place such as in the backyard or in an extra bedroom. Neighbors are likely to complain if you create a mess or potential safety hazards they can see.

Replace broken windows at once, and make sure the house is secure. You do not want vandals or curious children inside the property. Once the house is emptied, you can alleviate most odors by airing it out for a few days and by spreading baking soda over the plywood floors.

A "Primer" on Painting

After the property is cleaned up, the painting should be done. Once you have completed any needed drywall repairs, caulk any areas with gaps or cracked paint between moldings, windows, or corners. In addition to caulk, other useful products include construction adhesives such as Liquid Nails and Durhams Wood Repair Putty. Prior to painting, make sure all windows are operable. Use an oil-based, stain-blocking primer to cover dark walls, greasy stains, or smoke damage.

Paints are available in various sheens, from flat to high gloss. While glossy paint looks nice, it shows flaws in the walls; flat paint is dull, but it hides flaws. Most paint manufacturers sell satin or eggshell finishes, which are between flat and semigloss. Whatever you do, don't buy the cheapest paint—it will cost you double the labor for the extra coats! Purchase the major brands offered at the home-improvement stores and paint-store chains.

In less-expensive neighborhoods, you can paint over paneling if it is in decent condition. Caulk the seams and nail holes, prime, then reapply caulk to the areas you missed before painting. Copy what builders are doing in the newly constructed houses: Use light beige for all the wood trim and paint the doors white. If the base trim is worn, cracked, or just plain ugly, replace it with preprimed trim that costs less than 50¢ per linear foot.

Rent an airless paint sprayer for painting an entire house with no carpets. Complete the priming and other prep work and mask areas as needed. You can paint a 1,200-square-foot house in a few hours once the prep work is done. You may even be able to paint the inside and outside of the house on the same day. Eventually, you can buy your own sprayer. Plan on spending at least a thousand dollars for a commercial unit. The less-expensive consumer units are not as reliable or as fast as the quality units.

Move On to the Exterior Projects

Once you have cleaned up and painted the inside (and completed any other permit-less, low-profile projects), you can begin work on the property's exterior. Again, remember that once you start on the outside, you may get potential buyers interested, so don't start on the outside until the inside is cleaned and painted. The inside need not be finished at this point, but it should be presentable.

Replace damaged trim and siding and repair any other unsightly places on the home's exterior. Use paintable exterior caulk and scraping where necessary to prep the exterior for paint. Brick and stucco cracks and mortar problems can be repaired with the help of a professional. Repair gutters and downspouts, then the roof as needed.

Landscaping is important while mostly labor-intensive. Begin regularly watering the lawn immediately upon starting a new project and try to salvage existing plants. As mentioned earlier, keep it simple and tidy.

Finishing Up the Project

Assuming this is your first project, you should be almost complete with your renovations. Install the sinks, faucets, vanities, countertops, toilets, and other hardware. Paint the trim, doors, and cabinets. When all the messy work is completed, let the carpet and vinyl installers do their jobs. And vacuum up the loose carpet pieces after the carpet installers leave (major pet peeve!).

Decorating Your Masterpiece

Once you finish the renovation process, you should have a sparkling clean "new" property to sell. However, it will probably lack character inside and may seem washed out with all the white paint, and each room may blend together in your buyer's mind.

Real estate agents usually assume vacant houses are owned by desperate sellers. Show buyers and their agents that you know what you are doing so they don't try to beat you up on price. Because your property will show well, buyers should realize that they need to offer a fair price if they want to buy your house. Occupied houses may or may not show well, and buyers feel like they are inconveniencing the sellers when visiting their homes. Even a home that is well decorated by the owner-occupants may clash with the buyer's taste.

Builders spend thousands of dollars with interior decorators because they know what sells properties. You can invest in decorations a little at a time. As a starting point, utilize nice doormats to each entrance. These mats are welcoming to visitors and will help protect carpets. In homes with floor coverings other than carpeting, use throw rugs throughout. With beautiful hardwood floors, the rugs should be used as accents, while larger rugs should hide unattractive floors.

As with paint, decorations should remain relatively neutral, although you can add some color. Try to maintain a decorating style that complements the architecture and the age of the home. There is no need to furnish a house with bedroom furniture or other large pieces. Keep things simple and uncluttered. A small table near the main entrance is a good place for brochures and real estate agents' business cards. The idea is to upgrade the appearance of the property so use furnishings typically found in more expensive homes. Don't shop at Ethan Allen, but try to find something a step above dorm-room furnishings. You can find accent pieces at discount stores and garage sales at reasonable prices. Vases, bowls with potpourri, and candlesticks are just a few ideas.

Buy a couple of floor lamps to place in bedrooms. Artificial plants are definitely worth purchasing, as long as they look authentic. Small plant stands will add appeal and keep the plants off the floor. The kitchen should have a set of dish towels, paper towels, and maybe some glass jars with colorful contents on the counters. Several windows can show off tinted glass vases or sun catchers to add warmth. The bathroom should also have matching towels, soap and tissue dispensers, and a candle or something else with a pleasant scent. A bathroom should have an attractive shower curtain, unless you want to show off an unusually nice tile surround. Place a few pictures, wall hangings, and a mirror or two throughout the house, one item in each bedroom and two in the kitchen and family rooms. Hang the pictures on the walls, or lean them against the wall at floor level. Window shades give character to any house. Use them in the front windows and in other rooms that may have especially bad views, including finished basements.

Each room should be equipped with a light-sensing nightlight so that potential buyers can find their way around. You can place small handwritten signs throughout to point out various features. Visit show homes in new neighborhoods to gather ideas. You can even borrow a few items from your home if there is not too much sentimental attachment.

THE REHABBER'S TOOL KIT

Automobile

It's not practical to load your Geo Metro or new Cadillac up with building materials on a daily basis. Serious investors either drive trucks or have employees that do. You don't need to buy a brand new vehicle today. However, transporting your materials and equipment will eventually become an issue.

Practical Tip

Under Section 179 of the Internal Revenue Code, you can deduct the price of your large pickup truck or SUV up to $19,000 of the purchase price. You must use it 50 percent or more in your business and it must exceed 6,000 pounds gross weight. You can take the full deduction in the year you purchase it, even if you financed it! ▪

Tools

You will also need to invest in tools if you plan on doing any work yourself. We prefer to buy rather than rent equipment to save time and eventually money. But, realizing you cannot buy everything at once, try to start with the basics and always invest in well-made, established name-brand tools. Power and hand tools are dangerous in their own right, especially if they are of questionable quality. Budget an extra few hundred dollars into each job to buy the tools you will need along the way. In a few years you will have the equipment to tackle most projects by yourself, or to supply your crew with what they need to do jobs safely and effectively.

Even if you never plan on rehabbing a property, you should keep a clipboard, tape measure, flashlight, screwdriver, and crowbar in your car for inspecting houses that are either boarded, abandoned, or have no electricity.

Safety Items

There are also a few safety-related items that you should own if you do rehab work. Safety glasses, hearing protection, gloves, and a charcoal canister respirator are very important for you and your crew to use. Let your crew know that you expect the work site to be cleaned daily, and that you won't tolerate nails left in scrap lumber or other careless habits. A simple injury to yourself or a worker can cost more than you might think. Take simple precautions, and it will pay off in the long run. You should also keep a five- or ten-pound dry chemical fire extinguisher at each job site.

Key Points to Remember

- Learn about repairs and what they cost.
- Learn to fix the right things that are consistent with the neighborhood.
- Be generous on the cosmetic items.
- Prepare your property for showings.

CHAPTER 10

Liability and Tax Issues

While you need not let legal and tax issues scare you away from going gung ho into real estate, be aware of these issues. There's an old saying: "Nothing is for sure, except death and taxes." In real estate, that can be changed to: "Nothing is for sure, except lawsuits and taxes." Inevitably, you will run into trouble with both lawsuits and taxes, so make sure you understand the issues and prepare yourself properly.

NEVER DO BUSINESS IN YOUR OWN NAME

We live in a litigious society. Attorneys advertise on billboards with slogans such as "Have You Been Injured? You May be Entitled to a Cash Award!" Eighty million lawsuits are filed every year, an average of 152 per minute. The chances are greater that you will be sued than you will be in the hospital in the next year. The United States has 70 percent of the world's lawyers, and almost

50,000 new law school graduates are entering the profession each year! More lawyers means more competition for clients, which leads to new and creative theories of liability. Nobody wants to accept responsibility for his own actions. Everybody is a victim.

You cannot expect to reduce your risk of getting sued to zero, but you can take steps to reduce your risk as much as possible. In any situation where your money is at risk, ask yourself if there is a better way. Know the legal and financial risks of the situations in which you place yourself, your business, your family, and your money.

Avoid Being a Sole Proprietor

Most people who go into business do so as a sole proprietor. This means that they are doing business as an individual or under a fictitious name or dba (doing business as). This scenario offers absolutely no lawsuit protection, not to mention poor tax benefits (see the tax section later in this chapter). If the business is sued, all the individual's personal assets are at risk. The best way to protect yourself is to avoid getting sued personally.

Consider a Corporation for Flipping Properties

For less than $100 in most states, you can form a corporation to do your business or trade. If properly maintained, a corporation will shield your personal assets if the business is sued or goes bankrupt. A corporation can also provide you with some tax benefits (see the tax section later in this chapter). Furthermore, a corporation gives you a more professional look when dealing with people in business.

The best news is that you can do it yourself. Call Legalwiz Publications tollfree at 800-655-3632 and order your copy of *How to Create a Bulletproof Corporation.*

DON'T OWN REAL ESTATE IN YOUR OWN NAME

You wouldn't walk around with a financial statement taped to your forehead would you? So why would you have your most valuable assets exposed to public scrutiny? Owning real estate in your own name is like walking around with a giant KICK ME sign taped to your back. In every county in the United States, copies of deeds to real estate are recorded in the public records. Anyone can go to the county courthouse or recorder's office and look up the owner of any property.

Even if you just flip properties, your name will continue to appear on public record, leaving an easy paper trail for everyone to follow. While a corporation will protect you from liability, it will not keep your affairs private.

Consider holding title to every property you purchase, even the ones you flip, in a land trust. A land trust is a revocable, living trust used to hold title to property. A trustee is appointed who is a dummy (in legal terms, a nominee) to hold title for your benefit. The trustee cannot reveal the identity of the beneficial owner of the trust, unless he is brought into court and forced to by a judge. The land trust requires no filing fees, no attorney's fees, and no tax reporting, so it is inexpensive and easy to use. Hold title to property in a separate trust so it will be difficult for the public (especially lawyers) to follow your trail.

The best news is that you can do it yourself. Call Legalwiz Publications toll-free at 800-655-3632 and order your copy of *Your Step-by-Step Guide to Land Trusts.*

DOING BUSINESS WITH PARTNERS

Doing business with a partner is even worse than doing business as a sole proprietor. A partnership is formed when two or more people decide to do business together for profit. It does not require a formal partnership agreement or filing any official documents, although it is often formed that way. A partnership can be created even if you did not intend to!

Here is the problem with partnerships: If your partner does something foolish, you are liable. If you allow your partner to commit the partnership to a contract, the partnership and its partners can be held liable for that debt. If your partner slanders another, commits a negligent act, or incurs a debt on behalf of the partnership, you are on the hook—*even if your partner files for bankruptcy!* This is the doctrine of "joint and several liability." Regardless of the percentage of fault between you and your partners, a judgment by a creditor for any tortious acts is 100 percent collectible from any one of the partners. Joint and several liability can be particularly disastrous if you are the silent partner with all the money.

Another problem is the accidental partnership. For instance, Harry finds a good business deal. He needs capital, so he approaches Fred. Fred agrees to invest with Harry. Fred is the silent partner. Harry deals with the public, referring to his "partner" Fred. Fred and Harry do business, make money, and part ways. A month later, Harry gets into financial trouble. Creditors come knocking on his door, but he has no money to pay. The creditors then come after his partner Fred. Is Fred liable? In some cases, the answer is "yes" if the public thought Harry and Fred were partners and Fred did nothing to stop Harry.

If you only want a one-shot deal with a partner, consider drafting a joint venture agreement (see the sample in the Appendix C). A joint venture is basically a partnership for a specific purpose. If you intend to do business with partners for the long term, consider forming a corporation or limited liability company.

BASIC TAXATION RULES OF REAL ESTATE TRANSACTIONS

The foolish entrepreneur is the one who waits until April 14 to file his taxes, then hands a shoebox full of receipts to his accountant. You must plan for your taxes at the beginning of the tax year and consult with your tax advisors throughout the year. People who say the tax system isn't fair are just ignorant of the rules. Taxes will eat up a large percentage of your money over your lifetime, so learn how to make the rules work for you!

Tax Issues for the Scout

The scout is essentially selling information, which is a personal service. This would be reported as ordinary income on Schedule C of her federal income tax return. She could deduct expenses related to this activity on her return to offset the income.

Tax Issues for the Dealer and the Retailer

The dealer who assigns a contract is not selling real estate, but rather selling a commodity. This would be reported as ordinary income on Schedule C of his federal income tax return. He could deduct expenses related to this activity on his return to offset the income.

The dealer who sells properties by double closing is selling real estate. If he sells a few properties here and there, he could report this income on Schedule D of his income tax return as a short-term capital gain. He can deduct expenses directly related to the acquisition and sale of the property. He cannot, however, deduct general business expenses on Schedule D. These must be reported on a Schedule C. This may open a Pandora's box, as discussed later in this chapter.

Don't Forget to File IRS Form 1099!

If you pay a scout for information or a dealer for an assignment of contract more than $600 in one year, you must send him or her an IRS Form 1099 by January 31 of the following tax year. You must send a copy of the forms to the IRS, along with IRS Form 1096 by February 28. ▪

If the seller takes a promissory note for all or part of the purchase price, he can elect to use the installment sales method under *IRC Section 453*. By using the installment method, the seller can spread out the tax on his profits over several years. In this fashion, the gain is taxed pro rata as it is received. An installment sale is defined under the Internal Revenue Code (the Code or IRC) as a disposition of property in which the seller receives one or more payments after the close of the tax year in which the sale occurred. Installment sales are reported on IRS Form 6252.

THE REAL ESTATE DEALER ISSUE

In Chapter 1, we specifically referred to the dealer as one who buys properties with the intent of reselling them. The IRS uses a similar definition of a real estate dealer. The capital gains and installment sales rules apply for principal residences and properties held for "productive use." *(IRC §1234.)* If you are actively buying and selling real estate on a regular basis, you may be considered a "dealer" in real estate properties. A dealer is one who buys with the intent of reselling rather than for investment. In our terms, this applies to both the dealer and the retailer. There is no magic formula for determining who an investor is and who a dealer is, but the IRS will balance a number of factors, such as:

- The purpose for which the property was purchased
- How long the property was held
- The amount of sales by the taxpayer in that year
- The amount of income from sales compared to taxpayer's other income
- How many deals the taxpayer made in that year
- The amount of gain realized from the sale

If the IRS pegs you as a dealer, then you cannot use the installment sales method under *IRC §453.* The installment sales will be disallowed and the entire paper profit is reported as ordinary income in the year of sale. Furthermore, the sale of property cannot be reported on Schedule D; it must be reported on Schedule C as inventory. Thus the gains from the sale of real estate will be subject to self-employment tax, which is currently 15.3 percent of the first $72,600. If the IRS recharacterizes this income several years after the transaction, you may also be subject to additional interest and possibly a penalty.

Avoid Schedule C

As you may have discerned by now, doing business on a Schedule C as a sole proprietor is not recommended. Your liability is unlimited, you are subject to self-employment tax on earnings, and your chances of being audited as a small business are higher than if you are incorporated. ▪

As discussed previously, you should consider forming a corporation to buy and flip your properties. An S corporation is fine to begin, but consider the tax benefits of a C corporation when your business gets going full time. As you can see, a good certified public accountant who is knowledgeable in real estate is a key player who you need on your team. Make sure that he has many real estate clients and/or owns investment real estate.

What Is an S Corporation?

An S corporation is one that files an election under subchapter S of the code by filing IRS Form 2553. The S corporation files an informational tax return and the profits and losses from its business flow through to the shareholders. A C corporation files a tax return and pays taxes on its profits. Distributions (called *dividends*) to the shareholders are taxed again on the shareholders' personal returns. Of course, a reinvestment of profits rather than a distribution will not result in double taxation. Also, corporate income tax rates are lower than personal rates, up to about $100,000. Thus, using a C corporation for flipping properties could save you money in taxes if you reinvest rather than distribute profits each year. One type of corporation is not necessarily better than the other; you need to review your personal situation with a qualified tax advisor to see what is best for you. ▪

INDEPENDENT CONTRACTOR LIABILITY

The IRS and your state department of labor are on the lookout for employers who don't collect and pay withholding taxes, unemployment, and/or workers' compensation insurance.

If you have employees that are "off the books," you are looking for trouble. If you get caught, you will have to pay withholding taxes and as much as a 25 percent penalty. Intentionally failing to file W-2 forms will subject you to a $100 fine per form. The fine for failing to complete Immigration and Naturalization Service (INS) Form I-9 is from $100 to $1,000 per form. The corporation will not shield you from liability in this case, either. All officers, directors, and/or responsible parties are personally liable for the taxes, and this obligation cannot be discharged in bankruptcy.

If you have people who do contract work for you on a per-diem basis, they may be considered employees by the IRS. If a worker fails to pay her estimated taxes, you may still be liable for withholding. If these workers are under your control and supervision and only do work for you, the IRS may consider them employees, even if *you* don't. If this happens, you may be liable for back taxes and penalties as described previously.

If you want to protect yourself, at a minimum you should:

- Hire only corporate contractors (or possess a business card and letterhead of an unincorporated contractor)
- Require proof of insurance (liability, unemployment, and workers' compensation) in writing
- Have a written contract or estimate on the worker's letterhead that states that he will work his own hours and that you will have no direct supervision over the details of the work (see the sample agreement in Appendix C)

- Have letters of reference from other people the contractor did work for in your file to show that he did not work solely for you
- File IRS Form 1099 for every worker to whom you pay more than $600 per year

In addition to possible tax implications, an independent contractor can create liability for you if a court determines that the contractor is your employee. For example, if your independent contractor is negligent and injures another, the injured party can sue you directly. If facts show that you exercised enough control over your contractor, a court may rule that this contractor is your employee for liability purposes. As you may know, an employer is vicariously liable for the acts of his employees (i.e., liable as a matter of law without proof of fault on the part of the employer). Make certain you follow these guidelines for hiring contractors, particularly the issue of control.

Finally, be aware under your state law which duties are considered inherently dangerous. These duties cannot be delegated to an independent contractor without liability on your part, regardless of whether the person you hire is considered an independent contractor or an employee.

Key Points to Remember

- Avoid doing business in your own name or as a sole proprietor.
- Learn tax rules regarding real estate, especially the dealer rules.
- Be mindful of the legal and tax implications of people you hire to do work.

CHAPTER 11

Getting Started

Whether you are new to real estate or have reached a plateau, this chapter will help jump-start your real estate investing career.

SURROUND YOURSELF WITH LIKE-MINDED PEOPLE

Creative real estate is nontraditional, which means that most people don't handle real estate this way. Thus, most people you speak with will tell you this method won't work. If you tell them you heard about the concept in a seminar or in a course you bought from a late-night television guru, they will laugh and call you gullible. Attorneys and other professionals will denounce it, because it sounds unusual. Keep in mind that these people are either threatened by their own lack of success or are looking to protect themselves.

The first thing you should do is join a local real estate investment association. A nationwide list of them can be found at

<www.creonline.com/clubs.htm>. These associations will help you keep your thoughts in the right place and prove that creative real estate really does work, despite the opinions of self-proclaimed consumer advocates. If you cannot find a group, form your own mastermind group that meets for breakfast once a week. If you don't know what a mastermind group is, you should read *Think & Grow Rich* by Napoleon Hill. If you already read it, read it again, again, and again!

BUILD A TEAM

Don't wait until you have a deal brewing to find the players. You need the following players on your team.

Real Estate Attorney

Finding a good attorney is difficult, because most attorneys are not investors or are not familiar with creative real estate transactions. Most attorneys will give you just enough advice to keep them from getting sued, but not enough advice to show you how to make more money out of a deal.

A good real estate attorney advises you of the risks, suggests alternative ways of handling a transaction, and charges a reasonable fee. A bad real estate attorney either says nothing, points out problems without offering solutions, or systematically kills deals.

Ask other investors in your area who they use as an attorney. When interviewing a potential attorney, ask the following questions:

- Do you own rental property?
- How many closings do you handle per year?

- What kind of unusual transactions have you dealt with recently?
- Have you conducted any foreclosures, double closings, or installment land contracts?

Get a feel for the experience and personality of the attorney. A good attorney on your side is worth her weight in gold.

Title or Escrow Company

A competent title or escrow company can make closings run smoothly for you. Avoid using the big-name companies. Find a small local one that caters to investors. Make sure they understand double closings. You can usually obtain a good recommendation on a title or escrow company from other investors by joining a real estate investment group. In some states, only attorneys perform closings, which can be a blessing or a nightmare (see the previous discussion regarding attorneys).

Tax Advisor

In our experience, most CPAs and accountants are rank amateurs regarding real estate transactions. Most firms hire clerical help during the tax season, so less-experienced personnel might prepare your return. Tax return preparation is the easier part of taxes; the hard (and more important) part is good planning and using aggressive strategies. Be voracious about reading information on how to save money on taxes. It is time well spent. Read *The Real Estate Investor's Tax Guide* by Vernon Hoven (Dearborn).

Choose an accountant, CPA, or tax lawyer who can help you plan your business taxes for the year. Consult with him whenever you have questions about an unusual transaction. Consider doing your own return using a computer program, such as TurboTax by Intuit.

Good Contractor/Handyman

A capable all-around contractor/handyman is essential to your success, especially if you do not have extensive rehab knowledge. You can find this person by looking in the Services directory of your newspaper. Interview several people to find one who will give you free estimates and who will know how to cut corners in all the right places. Ask other local investors for a recommendation.

Mortgage Broker

As a dealer, you won't need to borrow money. Once you start retailing, however, you may need cash to fund your deals. Be careful to find a mortgage broker who is savvy, creative, and experienced in working with investors.

Partner or Mentor

While this book is an excellent resource for getting started in flipping properties, it is not the exhaustive reference for every situation. You need to have partners and mentors to work with on your deals. There aren't too many cookie cutters; every situation is unique, and the more you can tap into other people's knowledge and experience, the less mistakes you will make. If you start out as a part-time investor, you can probably find a partner to be involved in your projects. This partner may already have a rehab property you can help with, or perhaps you can team up with a contractor or another investor to help with a property you find. Either way, you can look at your first projects as an apprenticeship that will allow you to "earn while you learn."

Look for a knowledgeable and trustworthy mentor. The investment business should be approached with integrity, and most of the people who continue to succeed do business in an ethical way. Finally, don't be a leech for information. Respect other people's time and be willing to pay for it.

ONLY TALK TO MOTIVATED SELLERS

This point is becoming repetitive, but it is important. Talking to unmotivated sellers is the biggest mistake beginning investors can make. They waste time talking to sellers who are marginally motivated. Even worse, they drive by the house and look for comps without even talking to the seller first! Never leave your home before speaking with the seller over the telephone.

BE PERSISTENT

Anyone who has ever been in sales will tell you that few deals are ever made on the first try. In fact, most deals are made after contacting a prospect for the fourth or fifth time. Never underestimate the value of hard work. Diligence is a key to success, regardless of your background.

Employ a follow-up system for potential deals. Consider a contact management software program that will schedule follow-ups and keep a running history of calls and conversations. If you don't (or won't) use a computer, buy a package of index cards. Write information on each card about the property, its owners, and conversations you have had with them. Stick them on a bulletin board on your wall for follow up. No matter how you do it, just remember to follow up.

TREAT REAL ESTATE AS A BUSINESS

People are lured to real estate because of the quick buck that it promises. Don't hold your breath, for you won't get rich quick. An overnight sensation usually takes about five years. More than 90 percent of the people who take a real estate seminar quit after three months. Flipping properties should be treated as a serious career. It takes months, even years for a business to cultivate customers and create a life of its own. You need to treat it like any other business.

Have a Plan

Don't just wander around looking for deals. Draw up a plan and follow it. Make x number of telephone calls per week. Spend x dollars a month on advertising. Make x number of offers per week. Pass out x number of business cards each day. Eventually, you will start to get lucky. Ironically, luck always happens to those who are at the right place at the right time. If you plan and persist, you will get lucky.

SHOULD YOU INVEST IN REAL ESTATE FULL TIME?

Many self-acclaimed real estate gurus state that everyone should quit their jobs and immediately jump into full-time real estate investing. They often claim incredible results from students with little experience. We would like to caution that life-changing decisions are not usually simple and that full-time investing is not for everyone. Let's discuss some pros and cons of full-time versus part-time investing.

The Full-Time Investor

Entering the real estate profession on a full-time basis offers several advantages over a part-time commitment. Being successful requires you to develop knowledge in many aspects of real estate, and more time focused on real estate leads to greater knowledge. The more your learn, the more you earn, because you need not rely on as many professional services or partners for help. You also can recognize a deal (or a dud) faster, which gives you more time to do more business or to spend with your family.

As a full-time investor, you work your own hours. When we say full time, we may mean as little as 20 hours per week if you are good at finding deals. The rest of your time can be spent pursuing other vocations or hobbies. Or, if you are so inspired, you can work 40 or more hours and use the extra cash flow to buy rental properties or diversify your holdings in the stock market. The point is that you must satisfy your cash flow needs before you can start investing your money.

One final point you should consider is whether you want to be self-employed. If you have always worked for someone else, being your own boss sounds very attractive. In some respects, this isn't quite the truth. Being your own boss means being an accountant, bookkeeper, stock clerk, receptionist, and office manager all in one. You have to deal with tax returns, payroll, office supplies, customer service, bills, and all the other hassles that come with a business. You don't have friends to chat with at the water cooler. You don't have paid health insurance, a company car, and a 401(k). You take your problems home with you every night.

Sound like fun? It is, once you learn how to manage your time and run your business. Being the master of your own life and career is well worth the other hassles of dealing with your own business.

The Part-Time Investor

The part-time investor holds a regular job. This may be by choice or for the time being until his real estate ventures are bringing in enough cash so he can quit his job. If it is the latter reason, don't quit your job because the real estate guru told you so. Quit your job when it is not worth the income that it brings you. In other words, if you are making more money per hour flipping properties on the side, you are at the point where your regular job is costing you money. Only then is it time to quit!

One of the advantages of starting out part time is that you can maintain your cash flow while learning the business. It may take weeks or possibly months to find your first deal. That same deal may take several months to turn around, especially if you decide to fix it and sell it retail. Think twice before telling your boss you're leaving; you will have plenty of time to make the career switch once you have acquired more real estate experience. You may, on the other hand, like your occupation. If so, continue to work at it, and invest in real estate on the side.

The best-case scenario, if you are married, is for one spouse to work a regular job. The other spouse works the real estate business for creating wealth, retirement income, and a nice college fund for the children. Of course, in today's market, you could be laid off due to unforeseen circumstances. If you earn additional income flipping houses and invest the proceeds in rental properties, you will be covered if your main income is lost. This is especially the case for married women who often forgo careers and raise families, only to find themselves divorced with no means of making a living. We don't want to sound cynical about marriage, but with a 50 percent divorce rate in America, it never hurts to have a system for making money.

Someone with a full-time job tends to have little free time to focus on real estate. A part-timer should learn most of the same skills as a full-timer. Thus, the key disadvantage to flipping properties on a part-time basis is that it takes sacrifice to learn the business. Something has to give; television, lazy weekends, hobbies, and even some family activities must be compromised. As with any education, time spent learning about real estate will bring its own rewards, especially if the people in your life understand your goals and your plan to achieve these goals. If you are married, make sure your spouse reads this material with you and participates in the fun process of making money.

KEEP EDUCATED

"If you think education is expensive, try ignorance." We are not sure who first said this, but we give her credit. If you think a particular book, home-study course, or training is expensive, ask yourself, "Compared to what?" You will lose more money with a mistake than you will by learning how to avoid one.

Remember, the time you spend studying is time well spent. Don't buy something just to use it as a paperweight. No matter what the price of a book, seminar, or training program, it is always worth it if you put it to use and make money. However, the corollary to this statement is also true: A $20 book is a waste of money if you don't apply anything you learned from it (or if you didn't even read it!).

Study hard, apply yourself, and, above all, make some offers to purchase. You can't buy a property by studying everything about it. Too many people suffer from analysis paralysis when approaching a potential deal; they spend so much time going over minute details that they fail to take any action to purchase it. If you look at a potential real estate deal long enough, you will find enough reasons to talk yourself out of it for fear of losing your money. There is risk in every venture, but eventually you have to take a chance and just do it!

Key Points to Remember

- Treat real estate like a business—follow a plan.
- Be persistent in following up on leads.
- Assemble a team of experts.
- Engage a mentor.
- Keep educated, but take action!

Glossary

Abstract of Title A compilation of the recorded documents relating to a parcel of land, from which an attorney may give an opinion as to the condition of title. Also known in some states as a *preliminary title report.*

Acceleration A condition in a financing instrument giving the lender the power to declare all sums owed the lender immediately due and payable upon an event such as sale of the property.

Acre An area that contains 43,560 square feet of land. Also known as a *due-on-sale.*

Acknowledgment A declaration made by a person signing a document before a notary public or other officer.

Addendum An addition to a contract or agreement that adds more provisions or modifies provisions of the contract or agreement.

Adverse Possession Most states have laws that permit someone to claim ownership of property that is occupied for a number of years. This is common where a fence is erected over a boundary line (called an *encroachment*) without the objection of the rightful owner. After a number of years, the person who erected the fence may be able to commence a court proceeding to claim ownership of the property.

Agency A relationship in which the agent is given the authority to act on behalf of another person.

All-Inclusive Deed of Trust See *wraparound mortgage.*

ALTA American Land Title Association.

Amortize To reduce a debt by regular payments of both principal and interest.

Appraised Value The value of a property at a given time, based on facts regarding the location, improvements, etc., of the property and surroundings.

Appreciation An increase in the net value of real estate.

Appurtenance Anything attached to the land or used with it, passing to the new owner upon sale.

ARM An adjustable-rate mortgage; that is, a loan whose interest rate may adjust over time depending on certain factors or a predetermined formula.

Arrears Payment made after its due is in arrears. Interest is said to be paid in arrears because it is paid to the date of payment rather than in advance.

Assignment of Contract A process by which a person sells, transfers, and/or assigns rights under an agreement. Often used in the context of the assignment of a purchase contract by a buyer or the assignment of a lease by a tenant.

Assumable Loan A loan secured by a mortgage or deed of trust containing no due-on-sale provision. Most pre-1989 FHA loans and pre-1988 VA loans are assumable without qualification. Some newer loans may be assumed with the express permission of the note holder.

Assumption of Mortgage Agreement by a buyer to assume the liability under an existing note secured by a mortgage or deed of trust.

Attorney-in-fact An agency relationship in which a person holds a power of attorney allowing him or her to execute legal documents on behalf of another.

Bankruptcy A provision of federal law whereby a debtor surrenders assets to the bankruptcy court and is relieved of the obligation to repay unsecured debts. After bankruptcy, the debtor is discharged and unsecured creditors may not pursue further collection efforts against him or her. Secured creditors continue to be secured by property but may not take other action to collect.

Balloon Mortgage A note calling for periodic payments that are insufficient to fully amortize the face amount of the note prior to maturity, so that a principal sum known as a *balloon* is due at maturity.

Basis The financial interest one has in a property for tax purposes. Basis is adjusted down by depreciation and up by capital improvements.

Beneficiary One for whose benefit trust property is held. Also known as the lender under a deed of trust.

Binder A report issued by a title insurance company setting forth the condition of title and setting forth conditions that, if satisfied, will cause a policy of title insurance to be issued. Also known as a *title commitment.*

Building Restriction Line A required set-back a certain distance from the road within which no building may take place. This restriction may appear in the original subdivision plat, in restrictive covenants, or by building codes and zoning ordinances.

Buyer's Agent A real estate broker or agent who represents the buyer's interests, though typically the fee is a split of the listing broker's commission. Also known as the *selling agent.*

Capital Gain Profit from the sale of a capital asset, such as real property. A long-term capital gain is a gain derived from property held more than 12 months. Long-term gains can be taxed at lower rates than short-term gains.

Caveat Emptor Buyer beware. A seller is under no obligation to disclose defects, but may not actively conceal a known defect or lie if asked.

Certificate of occupancy A certificate issued by a local governmental body stating that the building may be occupied.

Chain of Title The chronological order of conveyancing of a parcel of land, from the original owner to the present owner.

Closing The passing of a deed or mortgage, signifying the end of a sale or mortgage of real property. Also known in some areas as *passing papers* or *closing of escrow.*

Cloud on Title An uncertainty, doubt, or claim against the rights of the owner of a property, such as a recorded purchase contract or option.

Commitment A written promise to make or insure a loan for a specified amount and on specified items. Also used in the context of title insurance *(title commitment).*

Community Property In community property states (Arizona, California, Idaho, Louisiana, Nevada, New Mexico, Texas, Washington, Wisconsin), all property of husband and wife acquired after the marriage is presumed to belong to both, regardless of how it is titled.

Comparables Properties used as comparisons to determine the value of a specified property.

Condominium A structure of two or more units, the interior spaces of which are individually owned. The common areas are owned as tenants in common by the condominium owners, and ownership is restricted by an association.

Contingency The dependence on a stated event that must occur before a contract is binding. Used both in the context of a loan and a contract of sale.

Contract of Sale A bilateral (two way) agreement wherein the seller agrees to sell and buyer agrees to buy a certain parcel of land, usually with improvements. Also used to reference to an installment land contract.

Contract for Deed See *installment land contract.*

Counteroffer A rejection of a seller's offer, usually with an amended agreement to sell the property to the potential buyer on different terms from the original offer.

Closing A meeting between the buyer, seller, and lender, or their agents, where the property and funds legally change hands.

Closing Costs Expenses incurred in the closing of a real estate or mortgage transaction. Most fees are associated with the buyer or borrower's loan. Closing costs typically include an origination fee, discount points, appraisal fee, title search and insurance, survey, taxes, deed recording fee, credit report, and notary fees.

Cloud on Title Any evidence of encumbrances.

Condemnation A judicial proceeding through which a governmental body takes ownership of a private property for a public use.

Collateral Property that is pledged to secure a loan.

Condominium A system of individual ownership of portions or units in a multiunit structure, combined with joint ownership of common areas. Each individual may sell or encumber his or her own unit.

Conventional Mortgage A loan neither insured by the FHA nor guaranteed by the VA.

Contract A legally enforceable agreement between two or more parties.

Cooperative Apartment A cooperative is a corporation that holds title to the land and building. Each co-op owner has shares of stock in the corporation that corresponds to an equivalent proprietary lease of an apartment space. Co-ops were very popular in New York City at one time, but are less common because of their lack of marketability due to high association fees.

Credit Report A report documenting the credit history and current status of a person's credit.

Deficiency The difference between the amount owed to a note holder and the proceeds received from a foreclosure sale. The lender may, in some states, obtain a *deficiency judgment* against the borrower for the difference.

Delivery The transfer of a deed to the grantee so that the grantor may not revoke it. A deed, signed but held by the grantor, does not pass title.

Depreciation Decrease in value to real property improvements caused by deterioration or obsolescence.

Documentary Tax Stamps Stamps, affixed to a deed, showing the amount of transfer tax. Some states simply charge the transfer tax without affixing stamps. Also known as *doc stamps*.

Double Closing A closing wherein a property is bought and then sold simultaneously. Also called *double escrow* and *flipping*.

Due-on-Sale Clause A provision in a mortgage or deed of trust that gives the lender the option to require payment in full of the indebtedness on transfer of title to the property (or any interest therein).

Earnest Money A good faith deposit or down payment.

Easement An interest that one has in the land of another. May be created by grant, reservation, agreement, prescription, or necessary implication.

Eminent Domain A constitutional right for a governmental authority to acquire private property for public use by condemnation, and the payment of just compensation.

Encroachment Construction or imposition of a structure onto the property of another.

Encumbrance A claim, lien, or charge against real property.

Equity The difference between the market value of the property and the homeowner's mortgage debt.

Equitable Title The interest of the purchase under an installment land contract.

Escrow Delivery of a deed by a grantor to a third party for delivery to the grantee on the happening of a contingent event.

Escrow Agent, Escrow Company Individual or company that performs closing services for real estate loans and sales transactions.

Escrow Payment That portion of a borrower's monthly payment held in trust by the lender to pay for taxes mortgage insurance, hazard insurance, lease payments, and other items as they become due. Also know as *impounds*.

Estate From the English feudal system, this defines the extent of one's ownership in a property.

Estate for Years An estate limited to a term of years. An estate for years is commonly called a *lease*. On the expiration of the estate for years, the property reverts back to the former owner.

Fee Simple The highest form of ownership. An estate under which the owner is entitled to unrestricted powers to dispose of the property, and which can be left by will or inherited. Also known as *fee* or *fee simple absolute*.

Federal Housing Administration (FHA) A federal agency that insures first mortgages, enabling lenders to loan a very high percentage of the sale price.

Fixture An item of personal property attached to real property.

Freddie Mac (FHLMC) Federal Home Loan Mortgage Corporation. A federal agency purchasing first mortgages, both conventional and federally insured, from members of the Federal Reserve System, and the Federal Home Loan Bank System.

Foreclosure A proceeding to extinguish all rights, title, and interest of the owner(s) of property in order to sell the property to satisfy a lien against it. About half of the states use a mortgage foreclosure, which is a lawsuit in court. About half use a power of sale proceeding, which is dictated by a deed of trust and is usually less time-consuming.

Ginnie Mae (GNMA) Government National Mortgage Association. A federal association working with FHA that offers special assistance in obtaining mortgages, and purchases mortgages in a secondary capacity.

Good Faith Estimate A lender's estimate of closing costs and monthly payment required by RESPA.

Grant Deed A deed commonly used in California to convey title. By law, a grant deed gives certain warranties of title.

Grantee A person receiving an interest in property.

Grantor A person granting or giving up an interest in property.

Grantor/Grantee Index The most common document recording indexing system is by grantor (the person conveying an interest, usually the seller or mortgagor) and grantee (the person receiving an interest, usually the buyer or mortgagee). All documents conveying property or an interest therein (deed, mortgage, lease, easement, etc.) are recorded by the grantor's last name in the grantor index. The same transaction is cross-indexed by the grantee's last name in the grantee index.

Heirs and Assigns Words usually found in a contract or deed that indicate that the obligations assumed or interest granted or binding upon or insure to benefit of the heirs or assigns of the party.

Homeowners Association An association of people who own homes in a given area for the purpose of improving or maintaining the quality of the area. Also used in the context of a condominium association.

Impound Account Account held by a lender for payment of taxes, insurance, or other payments. Also known as an *escrow* account.

Installment Land Contract The ILC is an agreement wherein the buyer makes payments in a manner similar to a mortgage. The buyer has equitable title. However, the seller holds legal title to the property until the contract is paid off. The buyer has equitable title, and, for all intents and purposes, is the owner of the property. Also known as a *contract for deed* or *contract of sale*.

Installment Sale A sale that involves the seller receiving payments over time. The Internal Revenue Code contains specific definitions and promulgates specific rules concerning installment sales and tax treatment of them. Also known as an *owner carry* sale.

Insured Mortgage A mortgage insured against loss to the mortgagee in the event of default and failure of the mortgaged property to satisfy the balance owing plus costs of foreclosure.

Interest Rate The percentage of an amount of money that is paid for its use for a specified time.

Joint and Several Liability A liability that allows a creditor to collect against any one of the debtors for the entire amount of the debt, regardless of fault or culpability. Most mortgage notes that are signed by husband and wife create joint and several liability.

Joint Tenancy An undivided interest in property, taken by two or more joint tenants. The interests must equal, accruing under the same conveyance, and beginning at the same time. On death of a joint tenant the interest passes to the surviving joint tenants, rather than to the heirs of the deceased.

Judgment The decision of a court of law. Money judgments, when recorded, become a lien on real property of the defendant.

Junior Mortgage Mortgage of lesser priority than the previously recorded mortgage.

Land Lease Owners of property will sometimes give long-term leases of land up to 99 years. A lease of more than 99 years is considered a transfer of fee simple. Land leases are commonly used to build banks, car lots, and shopping malls.

Land Trust A revocable, living trust primarily used to hold title to real estate for privacy and anonymity. Also known as an *Illinois land trust* or *nominee trust*. The land trustee is a nominal title holder, with the beneficiaries having the exclusive right to direct and control the actions of the trustee.

Lease/Option An agreement by which the lessee (tenant) has the unilateral option to purchase the leased premises from the lessor (landlord). Some lease/option agreements provide for a portion of the rent to be applied towards the purchase price. The price may be fixed at the beginning of the agreement or be determined by another formula, such as an appraisal at a later time. Also referred to as a *lease/purchase.*

Lease/Purchase Often used interchangeably with the expression *lease/option,* but technically means a lease in conjunction with a bilateral purchase agreement. Often used by real estate agents to mean a purchase agreement whereby the tenant takes possession prior to close of escrow.

Lien An encumbrance against property for money, either voluntary (e.g., mortgage), involuntary (e.g., judgment), or by operation of law (e.g., property tax lien).

Life Estate An estate in real property for the life of a living person. The estate then reverts back to the grantor or to a third party.

Lis Pendens A legal notice recorded to show pending litigation relating to real property and giving notice that anyone acquiring an interest in said property subsequent to the date of the notice may be bound by the outcome of the litigation. Often filed prior to a mortgage foreclosure proceeding.

License An authority to do a particular act or series of acts upon the land of another without possessing any estate or interest therein (e.g., a ski lift ticket). A license is similar to an easement in that it gives someone permission to cross property for a specific purpose. An easement is a property interest, whereas a license is a contractual right.

Liquidated Damages A contract clause that limits a party to a certain sum in lieu of actual damages. In the case of a real estate purchase and sale contract, the seller's legal remedy is limited to the buyer's earnest money deposit.

Loan-to-Value Ratio The ratio of the mortgage loan amount to the property's appraised value (or the selling price whichever is less).

Metes and Bounds A method of describing land by directions and distances rather than reference to a lot number.

Market Analysis A report estimating the resale value of a property. Usually prepared by a real estate agent showing comparable sales of properties in the vicinity based on tax records and information from the Multiple Listing Service.

Marketable Title Title that can be readily marketed to a reasonably prudent purchaser aware of the facts and their legal meaning concerning liens and encumbrances.

Mechanic's Lien A lien created by state law for the purpose of securing priority of payment for the price of value of work performed and materials furnished in construction or repair of improvements to land, and which attach to the land as well as the improvements.

Mortgage A voluntary lien filed against property to secure a debt.

Mortgage Broker One who, for a fee, brings together a borrower and lender, and handles the necessary applications for the borrower to obtain a loan against real property by giving a mortgage or deed of trust as security.

Mortgagee A lender.

Mortgagor A borrower.

Mortgage Guaranty Insurance Corporation (MGIC) A private corporation that, for a fee, insures mortgage loans similar to FHA and VA insurance, although not insuring as great a percentage of the loan.

Mortgage A security instrument given by a borrower to secure performance of payment under a note. The document is recorded in county land records, creating a lien (encumbrance) on the property. Also known as a *deed of trust* in some states. The borrower is also called a *mortgagor.*

Mortgage Insurance Insurance required for loans with a loan-to-value ratio above 80 percent. Also called PMI or MIP.

Multiple Listing Service A service performed by the Local Board of REALTORS® that provides information to aid in the sale of properties to a wide market base.

Notary Public One authorized by law to acknowledge and certify documents and signatures as valid.

Note A written promise to repay a certain sum of money on specified terms. Also known as a *promissory note.*

Offer A proposal to buy.

Option The unilateral right to do something. For example, the right to renew a lease or purchase a property. The optionee is the holder of the option. The optionor is the grantor of the option. The optionor is bound by the option, but the optionee is not.

Origination Fee A fee or charge for work involved in the evaluation, preparation, and submission of a proposed mortgage loan. Usually about 1 percent of the loan amount.

Payoff Amount A total amount needed to satisfy full payment on an existing loan or lien.

Performance Mortgage A mortgage or deed of trust given to secure performance of an obligation other than a promissory note.

Periodic Tenancy An estate from week-to-week, month-to-month, etc. In the absence of a written agreement (or on the expiration of a lease once payments are accepted), a periodic tenancy is created. Either party can terminate this type of arrangement by giving notice, usually equal to the amount of the period, or as prescribed by state law.

PITI Principal, interest, taxes, and insurance.

Plat A map showing the division of a piece of land.

Points Fee paid by a borrower to obtain a loan. A point is 1 percent of the principal amount of the loan. The borrower may usually pay more points to reduce the interest rate of the loan.

Power of Attorney A written document authorizing another to act on one's behalf as an attorney in fact.

Prepayment Penalty An additional charge imposed by the lender for paying off a loan before its due date.

Probate A court process to prove a will is valid.

Promissory Note A written, unsecured note promising to pay a specified amount of money on demand, often transferable to a third party.

Prorate To divide in proportionate shares. Used in the context of a closing, at which such things as property taxes, interest, rents, and other items are adjusted in favor of the seller, buyer, or lender.

Purchase Agreement A binding agreement between parties for the purchase of real estate.

Purchase Money Mortgage A loan obtained in conjunction with the purchase of real estate.

Quiet Title Proceeding A court action to establish or clear up uncertainty as to ownership to real property. Often required if a lien or cloud appears on title that cannot be resolved.

Quit Claim Deed A deed by which the grantor gives up any claim he or she may have in the property. Often used to clear up a cloud on title.

Real Estate Land and anything permanently affixed to the land, and those things attached to the buildings.

Real Property Land and whatever by nature or artificial annexation is attached to it.

REALTOR® Any member of the National Association of REALTORS®.

Recording The act of publicly filing a document, such as a deed or mortgage.

Recourse Note A note under which the holder can look personally to the borrower for payment.

Redemption The right, in some states, for an owner of lien holder to satisfy the indebtedness due on a mortgage in foreclosure after sale.

Refinancing The repayment of a loan from the proceeds of a new loan using the same property as collateral.

Reissue Rate A discounted charge for a title insurance policy if a previous policy on the same property was issued within a specified period (usually three to five years).

Release An instrument releasing a lien or encumbrance (e.g., mortgage) from a property.

RESPA (Real Estate Settlement Procedures Act) A federal law requiring disclosure of certain costs in the sale of residential property that is to be financed by a federally insured lender. Also requires that the lender provide a good faith estimate of closing costs prior to closing of the loan.

Second Mortgage A loan secured by a mortgage or trust deed, which lien is junior to a first mortgage or deed of trust.

Secondary Mortgage Market The buying and selling of first mortgages and deeds of trust by banks, insurance companies, government agencies, and other mortgagees.

Security Instrument A document under which collateral is pledged (e.g., mortgage).

Settlement Statement A statement prepared by a closing agent (usually a title or escrow company) giving a complete breakdown of costs and charges involved in a real estate transaction. Required by RESPA on a form HUD-1.

Special Assessment Tax imposed by the local government for public improvements, such as new streets.

Special Warranty Deed A seller warrants he or she has done nothing to impair title but makes no warranty prior to his or her ownership.

Specific Performance An action to compel the performance of a contract.

Subdivision Dividing land into lots and streets, typically under strict requirements of the state and county.

Sublet To let part of one's estate in a lease. A subtenant is not in privity of contract with the landlord and neither can look to each for performance of a lease agreement.

Subject-To When transferring title to a property encumbered by a mortgage lien without paying off the debt or assuming the note, the buyer is taking title "subject to."

Subordination The process by which a lien holder agrees to permit a lien to become junior or subordinate to another lien.

Tenancy in Common With tenancy in common, each owner (called a *tenant*) has an undivided interest in the possession of the property. Each tenant's interest is salable and transferable. Each tenant can convey that interest by deed, mortgage, or will. Joint ownership is presumed to be in common if nothing further is stated on the deed.

Tenancy by the Entirety A form of ownership recognized in some states by which husband and wife each owns the entire property. As with joint tenancy, in event of death of one, the survivor owns the property without probate. In some states, tenancy by entirety protects the property from obligations of one spouse.

Testate When a person dies with a will.

Title Title is the evidence of ownership. In essence, title is more important than ownership because having proper title is proof of ownership. If you have a problem with your title, you will have trouble proving your ownership and thus selling or mortgaging your property.

Title Insurance An insurance policy that protects the insured (purchaser and/or lender) against loss arising from defects in title. A policy protecting the lender is called a *loan policy*, whereas a policy protecting the purchaser is called a *owner's policy*. Virtually all transactions involving a loan require title insurance.

Title Search An examination of the public records to disclose facts concerning the ownership of real estate.

Truth in Lending Federal law requiring, among other things, a disclosure of interest rate charges and other information about a loan.

Trust A right to or in property held for the benefit of another, which may be written or implied.

Trustee One who holds property in trust for another party.

Trustor One who creates a trust by granting property to a trustee. Also known as the *borrower* on a deed of trust.

VA Loan A long-term, low or no down-payment loan guaranteed by the Department of Veterans Affairs, which is offered to individuals qualified by military service or other entitlements.

Warranty Deed A deed under which the seller makes a guarantee or warranty that title is marketable and will defend all claims against it.

Wraparound Mortgage A mortgage that is subordinate to and incorporates the terms of an underlying mortgage. The mortgagor (borrower) makes payments to the mortgagee (lender), who then makes payments on an underlying mortgage. Also referred to as an *all-inclusive deed of trust* in some states.

Yield Spread Premium A kickback from the lender to the mortgage broker for the additional profit made from marking up the interest rate on a loan.

Zoning Regulation of private land use and development by a local government.

Good Deal Checklist

If you answer no to one or two of these questions, then carefully reconsider purchase of the selected property. If you answer no to three of these questions, then do not do the deal. As a beginner you should leave it for someone willing to take a large risk. Perhaps you can sell your contract to another investor with different needs or goals.

- Would I feel safe here at night?
- Does the house fit in with others in the neighborhood?
- Is the house in a residential neighborhood (more houses than businesses or apartments)?
- Is the house worth saving?
- Would the house conform to FHA lending guidelines after renovations?
- Is the purchase price 25 percent less than similar homes have sold for in the neighborhood?
- Could I complete renovations in less than two months?

- Could I pay someone less than $25,000 to bring it up to satisfactory condition?
- Is the average property listed for sale in the area selling in less than 90 days?
- Would the house make a good starter home for a family?
- Are there several boarded-up houses on the block?
- Can I fully inspect prior to closing?
- Will the owner deliver the property with a general warranty deed?

APPENDIX B

Sample Ads

SAMPLE CLASSIFIED ADS TO BUY PROPERTIES

WE BUY HOUSES ALL CASH
Fast Closing • Any Condition
Call Bob @ 303-555-5555

UGLY, VACANT AND FIXUP
PROPERTIES WANTED!
Any Area • Any Condition
Call Bob @ 303-555-5555

Do You Have a Problem House?
Let us buy it and solve your
problem. We can close in as
little as 3 days.
Call Bill @ 303-555-5555

PROPERTY NOT SOLD?
We'll Make You an Offer Right
Over the Phone! We are not
Real Estate Agents.
Call Bob @ 303-555-5555

SAMPLE CLASSIFIED ADS TO SELL PROPERTIES

FIXER PROPERTY FOR SALE
All cash terms. Serious
investors only.
Call Bob @ 303-555-5555

EL DUMPO!
Fixer property for sale cheap.
Call Bill @ 303-555-5555

NEEDS TLC - WILL SELL CHEAP
To first Investor with CASH.
Call Bob @ 303-555-5555

SAMPLE BUSINESS CARDS

REAL ESTATE SOLUTIONS, Inc.
We Buy Houses Fast and Solve Your Problems!

- Foreclosures
- Fixup properties
- Tax liens
- Divorce

There is no problem we can't solve!

Ira Investor, President

Call anytime - (555) 555-5555 • Cell # (555) 555-5555

WE BUY HOUSES CASH
FAST CLOSING - AS LITTLE AS 72 HOURS
ANY CONDITION ● ANY AREA

Real Estate Solutions, Inc.
Ira Investor, President
(555)555-5555

SAMPLE MARKETING POSTCARDS

Cash for Your House
No Brokers, No Banks, No B.S.!

Closing in as Little as 72 Hrs.
We are <u>Not</u> Real Estate Agents
Call (555) 555-5555

DO YOU NEED TO SELL YOUR PROPERTY FAST?

Is your property vacant or in need of repairs? Are you behind in payments? Do you have back taxes owed or other liens? Do you need cash right away?

Call Us Today! Guaranteed Offer Over the Phone.
Real Estate Solutions, Inc.
Ira Investor, President
(555)555-5555

SAMPLE FLIER

Cash for Your House
No Brokers, No Banks, No B.S.!

Closing in as Little as 72 Hrs.
We are <u>Not</u> Real Estate Agents

Referral Fees Paid for Leads - Earn as much as $500 per week!
Call (555) 555-5555

SAMPLE DOOR HANGER

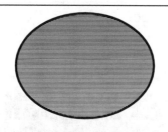

CASH FOR YOUR HOUSE!

No Brokers, No Banks, No B.S.!

Closing in as Little as 72 Hrs. We are <u>Not</u> Real Estate Agents!

Referral Fees Paid for Leads - Earn as much as $500 per week!

Call (555) 555-5555

SAMPLE MARKETING FAX TO REAL ESTATE AGENTS

Real Estate Solutions, Inc.   Tel (555) 555-5555
123 Main Street   (555) 555-5555
Anywhere, USA 12345

WE PAY CASH FOR
FIXER PROPERTIES!

Dear Real Estate Professional:

We are independent investors that pay cash for fixer properties in the
following areas:

- East Side
- West Side
- Roaring Fork

We can close quickly and for ALL CASH. If you come across fixer
properties in any of these areas, please call or fax the information to us and we
will make an offer.

Thank you for your time.

Ira Investor, President
Real Estate Solutions, Inc.

APPENDIX C

Sample Forms

Form Name	When to Use
Standard Contract	Pro-buyer contract when dealing with for-sale-by-owner
Addendum to Contract	Pro-buyer addendum to attach to a standard real estate contract. Not necessary when using the standard contract listed above.
Assignment of Contract	To assign your purchase contract to another investor
Authorization to Release Loan Information	Written permission to contact seller's lender for payoff information on a loan
Power of Attorney	Limited power of attorney for dealing with property that was quit-claimed to you in foreclosure
Due-on-Sale Acknowledgment	Have seller sign when you take a deed subject to an existing loan

Memorandum of Agreement	Affidavit used to cloud title to property to prevent seller from selling the property to someone else
Fax Offer	Sample fax offer to agent before contract
Quitclaim Deed	Give one whenever possible; it gives no warranty
Warranty Deed	Get one whenever possible; it has full warranties
Grant Deed	Used in California instead of a warranty deed
Appraisal Form	Excerpt from Uniform Residential Appraisal Report used by appraisers to determine value of property
Independent Contractor Agreement	Have all contractors you hire sign this form
Joint Venture Agreement	Used when doing a one-time partnership on a deal

AGREEMENT FOR PURCHASE
& SALE OF REAL ESTATE

AGREEMENT dated this __1st__ day of _____Feb_____ 20_00_ by and between

Mickey Motivated Seller

hereinafter "Seller" whose address is 123 Main St, Denver, CO 80203

and Real Estate Solutions, Inc.

hereinafter "Buyer" (and/or assigns or nominees) whose address is
Post Office Box 221, Denver, CO 80203

    1. THE PROPERTY. The parties hereby agree that Seller will sell and Buyer will buy the following property, located in and situate in the County of _Denver_ , State of _Colorado_ , to wit:

Lot 21, Block 12, Brighton Subdivision #1, City & County of Denver

known by street and address as _123 Main Street, Denver, CO 80203_

The sale shall also include all personal property and fixtures, except

Unless specifically excluded, all other items will be included, whether or not affixed to the property or structures. Seller expressly warrants that property, improvements, building or structures, the appliances, roof, plumbing, heating and/or ventilation systems are in good and working order. This clause shall survive closing of title.

    2. PURCHASE PRICE. The total purchase price to be paid by Buyer will be $50,000.00 payable as follows:

Non-refundable earnest money deposit (see below)	$ 500.00
Balance due at closing	$ 49,500.00
Owner financing from seller (see below)	$ 10,000.00
New loan (see below)	$ 39,500.00
Subject to existing loans	$ N/A

Said price is subject to appraisal by buyer and/or agent of buyer's choice.

    3. EARNEST MONEY. The buyer's earnest money shall be held in escrow by agent of buyer's choice. Upon default of this agreement, seller shall retain earnest money as his sole remedy without further recourse between the parties.

4. <u>NEW LOAN</u>. This agreement is contingent upon buyer's ability to obtain a new loan in the amount of $ _39,500.00_____. Buyer is not required to accept any loan with interest rate exceeding _10_____% amortized over _30_____years or pay any closing costs or points exceeding _$3,000_____. Buyer shall provide seller with written proof of a loan commitment on or before_Feb 25_____, 20_00

5. <u>SELLER FINANCING</u>. Buyer shall execute a promissory note in the amount of $ _10,000.00_____. In case of default, recourse shall be against the property an there shall be no personal recourse against the borrower. As security for performance of the promissory note, buyer shall provide the seller a mortgage, deed of trust or other customary security agreement which shall be subordinate to a new first mortgage not to exceed $ _40,000.00_____.

6. <u>EXISTING LOAN</u>. In the event part of the purchase price is to be satisfied by buyer taking subject to existing financing, buyer shall not be required to pay fees exceeding $_100.00_____ nor be required to show income or creditworthiness to the holder of said mortgage or deed of trust. Seller expressly agrees and understands that buyer is taking the property "subject to" such mortgages or deeds of trust, and is not expressly assuming responsibility for the underlying loans. If the actual loan balance of said loan is less than as stated herein, the purchase price shall be reduced to reflect the difference; if the actual loan balance is more than as stated herein, then buyer's required cash payment shall be reduced accordingly. Seller agrees to waives tax and insurance escrows held by said lender or its/assigns.

7. <u>CLOSING</u>. Closing will held be on or about _March 15_____, 20_00_, at a time and place designated by buyer. Buyer shall choose the escrow, title and/or closing agent. Seller agrees to convey title by a general warranty deed.

At closing, Buyer shall pay the following costs in transferring title:

[ ] title insurance policy [ ] loan assumption [ ] transfer fee [✓] transfer taxes [✓] recording fees [ ] title company closing, escrow and delivery charges [ ] hazard insurance premium [ ] mortgage insurance premium [ ] survey [ ] credit application.

The following Items will be prorated at closing:
[ ] Mortgage insurance [✓] Property taxes [ ] PMI Insurance [ ] Hazard insurance
[✓] Homeowner's association dues [✓] Rents [ ] Other _____

The buyer may extend the closing date an additional THIRTY (30) days by paying the seller $ _500.00_____in cash. Seller agrees to provide possession of the property free of all debris and in "broom clean" condition at closing. Buyer reserves the right to do a final "walk through" the day of closing.

8. <u>POSSESSION</u>. Seller shall surrender possession to the property in broom clean condition, and free of all personal items and debris on or before _March 15_, 20_00_ ("possession date", In the event possession is not delivered at closing, buyer shall withhold proceeds from the sale in the amount of $_700.00_____ as security. Seller shall be liable for damages in the amount of

$ _75.00_ per day for each day the property is occupied beyond the possession date. This paragraph shall survive the closing of title.

9. <u>EXECUTION IN COUNTERPARTS</u>. This agreement may be executed in counterparts and by facsimile signatures. This agreement shall become effective as of the date of the last signature.

10. <u>INSPECTION</u>. This agreement is subject to the final inspection and approval of the property by the buyer in writing on or before _March 15_, 20_00_.

11. <u>ACCESS</u>. Buyer shall be entitled a key and be entitled to access to show partners, lenders, inspectors and/or contractors prior to closing. Buyer may place an appropriate sign on the property prior to closing for prospective tenants and/or assigns.

Mickey Motivated Seller   *Feb 1, 2000*
Seller   Date

Seller   Date

Real Estate Solutions, Inc. by
Ira Investor, President   *Feb 1, 2000*
Buyer   Date

STATE OF *Colorado*   )
) ss:
COUNTY OF *Denver*   )

On _Feb 1st_, 20 _00_, before me, *Nancy Notary*, a notary public in and for said state personally appeared *Mickey Motivated Seller*, personally known to me (or proved to me based upon satisfactory evidence) to be the person(s) whose name(s) are subscribed to the within instrument and acknowledged that (s)he/they executed the same in his/her/their signature on the instrument the person(s) or entity on behalf of which they acted, executed the instrument.

Witness my hand and official seal

NOTARY SEAL

Nancy Notary
NOTARY PUBLIC
My commission expires *Jan 15, 2003*

CONTRACT ADDENDUM

Addendum to contract dated _____ Feb _____ 1st , 20_ 00

     Property Address: 123 Main Street, Denver, CO 80203

     Seller(s) Mickey Motivated Seller

     Buyer(s) Real Estate Solutions, Inc.

Notwithstanding anything to the contrary in the attached contract, the parties agree as follows:

<u>EARNEST MONEY</u>. The buyer's earnest money shall be held in escrow by agent of buyer's choice. Upon default of this agreement, seller shall retain earnest money as his sole remedy without further recourse between the parties.

<u>SELLER FINANCING</u>. In the event of any Seller financing, the promissory Note to be executed by the Buyer shall have no personal recourse against the borrower.

<u>EXISTING LOAN</u>. In the event part of the purchase price is to be satisfied by buyer taking subject to existing financing, buyer shall not be required to pay fees exceeding $ 100.00 _____ nor be required to show income or creditworthiness to the holder of said mortgage or deed of trust. Seller expressly agrees and understands that buyer is taking the property "subject to" such mortgages or deeds of trust, and is not expressly assuming responsibility for the underlying loans. If the actual loan balance of said loan is less than as stated herein, the purchase price shall be reduced to reflect the difference; if the actual loan balance is more than as stated herein, then buyer's required cash payment shall be reduced accordingly. Seller agrees to waives tax and insurance escrows held by said lender or its/assigns.

The buyer may extend the closing date an additional THIRTY (30) days by paying the seller $ 500.00 _____ in cash. Buyer reserves the right to do a final "walk through" the day of closing.

<u>POSSESSION</u>. Seller shall surrender possession to the property in broom clean condition, and free of all personal items and debris on or before March 15 , 20_ 00 ("possession date", In the event possession is not delivered at closing, buyer shall withhold proceeds from the sale in the amount of $ 700.00 _____ as security. Seller shall be liable for damages in the amount of $ 75.00 per day for each day the property is occupied beyond the possession date. This paragraph shall survive the closing of title.

<u>EXECUTION IN COUNTERPARTS</u>. This agreement may be executed in counterparts and by facsimile signatures. This agreement shall become effective as of the date of the last signature.

<u>INSPECTION</u>. This agreement is subject to the final inspection and approval of the property by the buyer in writing on or before ____ March 15 ____, 20_ 00 ___.

ACCESS. Buyer shall be entitled a key and be entitled to access to show partners, lenders, inspectors and/or contractors prior to closing. Buyer may place an appropriate sign on the property prior to closing for prospective tenants and/or assigns.

Mickey Motivated Seller	*Feb 1, 2000*
Seller	Date
Seller	Date
Real Estate Solutions, Inc. by	
Ira Investor, President	*Feb 1, 2000*
Buyer	Date

ASSIGNMENT OF CONTRACT

Real Estate Solutions, Inc. _____(hereinafter "Assignor"), the Buyer under an

agreement dated_____Feb____1st, 20____00____ (hereinafter "Agreement") by and between

Assignor and Mickey Motivated Seller_____(hereinafter "Seller"), hereby assigns

all right, title and interest in said agreement to Ronnie Retailer_____

(hereinafter "Assignee") for the sum and consideration of $ 3,500.00_____

received by Assignor.

    Assignee agrees to perform all covenants, conditions and obligations required by

Assignor under said Agreement and agrees to defend, indemnify and hold Assignor harmless

from any liability or obligation under said Agreement. Assignee further agrees to hold Assignor

harmless from any deficiency or defect in the legality or enforceability of the terms of said

agreement.

Dated this _1st_ day of _____Feb_____, 20____00_____

Real Estate Solutions, Inc. by
Ira Investor, President
_____
Assignor

Ronny Retailer
_____
Assignee

AUTHORIZATION TO RELEASE LOAN INFORMATION

Authorization dated this <u>1st</u> day of <u>Feb</u>, 20<u>00</u>

Borrower(s): <u>Mickey Motivated Seller</u>

Loan No.: <u>1234567</u>

Property: <u>123 Main Street, Denver, CO 80203</u>

TO: <u>Northwest Mortgage, PO Box 132, Fargo, ND 65434</u>

_____

_____

I/We the undersigned hereby authorize you to release information regarding the above-referenced loan to <u>Real Estate Solutions, Inc.</u>
and/or their agents/assigns. This form may be duplicated in blank and or sent via facsimile transmission. This authorization is a continuation authorization for said persons to receive information about my loan, including duplicates of any notices sent to me regarding my loan.

Mickey Motivated Seller
_____
Borrower

DOB: <u>3/10/62</u>

SSN: <u>234-345-6787</u>

_____
Borrower

DOB:_____

SSN: _____

LIMITED POWER OF ATTORNEY

KNOW ALL MEN BY THESE PRESENTS:

THAT, I, _____Mickey Motivated Seller_____, of the County of

_____Denver_____ State of _____Colorado_____, reposing special trust and

confidence in _Real Estate Solutions, Inc._____ (hereinafter "Agent"), of the County of

_____Denver_____, State of _Colorado_____

have made, constituted and appointed, and by these presents do make, constitute and appoint said Agent to be my true and lawful attorney-in-fact, to act for me and in my stead, and to sell and convey the following property (enter legal description below):
Lot 21, Block 12, Brighton Subdivision #1, City & County of Denver

or any interest in said land for such price as to my agent may seem advisable.

My agent is hereby authorized to sign, seal and deliver as my act and deed any contract, deed, or other instrument in execution of any agreement for sale made by me or my agent, in such manner that all my estate, right, title and interest in said land may be effectually and absolutely conveyed and assigned to the purchaser thereof, his, her, or its heirs, successors and assigns forever, or to such other person or entity as purchaser may name or appoint; and I hereby declare that any and all of the contracts, deeds, receipts or matters, and things which shall be by my said agent given, made or done for the aforesaid purposes shall be as good, valid and effectual as if they had been signed, sealed and delivered by me in my own proper person; and I hereby undertake at all times to ratify whatsoever my said agent shall lawfully do or cause to be done in or concerning the premises by virtue of these presents. My agent is hereby further authorized to receive the consideration or purchase price arising from the sale of such land or any interest therein, and to give good receipt therefore, which receipt shall exonerate the person paying such money to my agent from looking to the application, or being responsible for the loss or misapplication thereof. If said consideration should be paid by check or draft, my said agent is hereby authorized to endorse and cash said check or draft and collect the proceeds thereof, whether the same be made payable to me or to my agent, as my attorney-in-fact. My agent may contact and lender, lien holder or government authority regarding money or other obligations owed regarding the property and may further execute any and all documents necessary to correct any deficiency in previously executed documents regarding the ownership or sale of the property.

IN WITNESS WHEREOF, I have hereunto set my hand and seal this _1st_ day of _February_, 20 _00_.

Mickey Motivated Seller
_____
Principal's Name

Mickey Motivated Seller
_____
Principal's Legal Signature

STATE OF _Colorado_____, COUNTY OF _Denver_____)ss:

On _Feb 1st_, 20 _00_, before me, _Nancy Notary_____, a notary public in and for said state personally appeared
_Mickey Motivated Seller_____,
_____personally known to me (or proved to me based upon satisfactory evidence) to be the person(s) whose name(s) are subscribed to the within instrument and acknowledged that (s)he/they executed the same in his/her/their signature on the instrument the person(s) or entity on behalf of which they acted, executed the instrument.

Witness my hand and official seal

Nancy Notary_____
NOTARY PUBLIC
My commission expires _Jan 15, 2003_

DUE-ON-SALE ACKNOWLEDGEMENT

WHEREAS, _____Mickey Motivated Seller_____ as Seller and
_____Real Estate Solutions, Inc._____ as Purchaser have entered in to a certain
purchase and sales agreement even date herewith, the parties fully understand, acknowledge an
agree as follows:

1. Both Seller and Purchase are fully aware that the mortgage(s)/deeds of trust securing
the property located at 123 Main Street, Denver, CO contain(s) provisions prohibiting the
transfer of any interest in the property without satisfying the principal balance remaining on the
underlying loans and/or obtaining the lender's prior written consent (i.e., a "due-on-sale" clause),
and that this transaction may violate said mortgage. **Seller specifically understands that this
loan will be paid on a monthly basis by buyer, but will not be assumed or paid off
completely at this time, and that this loan will remain in Seller's name and may continue to
appear on Seller's credit report.**

2. Seller and Purchaser execute this disclosure form after having had the opportunity to
seek legal counsel as to the legal and financial implications of the due-on-sale clause. The
parties agree and understand that if said due on sale clause is enforced by the holders of said
mortgages, the entire balance due under said mortgages/deeds of trust will have to be paid off.
In this event, Seller and Purchaser agree to take all reasonable steps to satisfy said lender,
including both parties taking steps to obtain financing and/or Purchaser submitting an application
to formally assume liability for said obligations. Purchaser understands that in the event that the
underlying debt is not paid off, the lender holding the deeds of trust may foreclose the property
which will extinguish Purchaser's interest under the Installment Land Contract.

3. Seller and Purchaser hereby agreed to defend, indemnify and hold all parties involved
in this transaction harmless from any liability in the event that the holders of the mortgages
and/or deeds of trust on the aforementioned property are called due and payable.

Mickey Motivated Seller
_____   _____
Seller   Purchaser

On *Feb 1st*____, 20 *00* , before me, *Nancy Notary*____, a notary public in and for said state personally
appeared *Mickey Motivated Seller*____, personally known to me (or proved to me based upon satisfactory
evidence) to be the person(s) whose name(s) are subscribed to the within instrument and acknowledged that
(s)he/they executed the same in his/her/their signature on the instrument the person(s) or entity on behalf of which
they acted, executed the instrument.

Witness my hand and official seal

*Nancy Notary*_____
NOTARY PUBLIC
My commission expires *Jan 15, 2003*_____   [SEAL]

AFFIDAVIT AND MEMORANDUM OF
AGREEMENT CONCERNING REAL ESTATE

State of _____Colorado_____)
County of ___Denver_____) ss:

BEFORE ME, the undersigned authority, on this day personally appeared _Real Estate Solutions, Inc._____, who being first duly sworn, deposes and says that an agreement for the Purchase and Sale of the real property described as (enter legal description below): Lot 21, Block 12, Brighton Subdivision #1, City & County of Denver

was entered into by and between the undersigned Affiant, as Buyer, and _____ _____Mickey Motivated Seller_____, as Seller, on the ___1st___ day of _____Feb_____, 20__00__.

A copy of the agreement for purchase and sale of said real property may be obtained by contacting _Real Estate Solutions, Inc._____, whose mailing address is _Post Office Box 221, Denver, CO 80203_____, and whose telephone number is _(555) 555-5555_____.

Dated this ___1st___ day of _____Feb_____, 20__00__.

FURTHER AFFIANT SAYETH NOT.

AFFIANT'S NAME_Real Estate Solutions, Inc._____

AFFIANT'S SIGNATURE_*Mickey Motivated Seller*_____

On _*Feb 1st*___, 20 _00_, before me, _*Nancy Notary*_____, a notary public in and for said state personally appeared _*Mickey Motivated Seller*_____, personally known to me (or proved to me based upon satisfactory evidence) to be the person(s) whose name(s) are subscribed to the within instrument and acknowledged that (s)he/they executed the same in his/her/their signature on the instrument the person(s) or entity on behalf of which they acted, executed the instrument.

Witness my hand and official seal

*Nancy Notary*_____
NOTARY PUBLIC
My commission expires _*Jan 15, 2003*_____   [SEAL]

FAX OFFER TO PURCHASE

<u>TO</u>: Barney Broker
<u>FROM</u>: Ira Investor
<u>DATE</u>: January 29, 2000
<u>RE</u>: 1234 Main Street, Anywhere, USA, MLS Listing #12345

Dear Mr. Broker:

We are willing to submit a formal offer to purchase the above-referenced property for $110,000 cash and close on or before February 15th, 2000. This offer will expire if not accepted on or before 5:00 PM, February 1, 2000.

Please present this information verbally to your client.

Upon acceptance, we will submit a company check in the sum of $500 as earnest money and execute a formal real estate purchase contract.

This offer is subject to a complete inspection of the premises.

Ira Investor
_____
Ira Investor

----------------------------[Space Above Reserved for Recording Purposes]-----------------------

QUIT-CLAIM DEED

THIS QUIT-CLAIM DEED, is executed this ___1st___ day of ___Feb___, 20__00__ by

Mickey Motivated Seller
_____ hereinafter referred to as "First Party", to

Real Estate Solutions, Inc.
_____ hereinafter referred to as "Second Party", whose

address is _Post Office Box 221, Denver, CO 80203_____.

WITNESSETH, that the First Party, for and in consideration of the sum of $10.00 and other good and valuable consideration in hand paid by the said Second Party, the receipt whereof is hereby acknowledged, does hereby remise, release and quit-claim unto the Second Party, all right, title, interest, and claim which the First Party has in and to the following described lot, piece or parcel of land, situate, lying and being in the county of _____Denver_____, State of _____Colorado_____ to wit:

Lot 21, Block 12, Brighton Subdivision #1, City & County of Denver

Also known as street and number as _123 Main Street, Denver, CO 80203_____.

TO HAVE AND HOLD the same, together with all and singular the appurtenances thereunto, of all interest, equity and claim whatsoever the First Party may have, either in law or equity, for the proper use, benefit and behalf of the Second Party forever.

IN WITNESS WHEREOF, the First Party has signed and sealed these presents the day and year first above written.

Mickey Motivated Seller
_____   _____
First Party   First Party

STATE OF *Colorado*_____, COUNTY OF *Denver*_____)ss:

On _*Feb 1st*_____, 20_*00*__, before me, *Nancy Notary*_____, a notary public in and for said state personally appeared *Mickey Motivated Seller*_____, personally known to me (or proved to me based upon satisfactory evidence) to be the person(s) whose name(s) are subscribed to the within instrument and acknowledged that (s)he/they executed the same in his/her/their signature on the instrument the person(s) or entity on behalf of which they acted, executed the instrument.

Witness my hand and official seal

Nancy Notary
_____
NOTARY PUBLIC
My commission expires *Jan 15, 2003*_____   [NOTARY SEAL]

------------------------------[Space Above Reserved for Recording Purposes]------------------------

WARRANTY DEED

THIS DEED, made this __1st__ day of _____ Feb _____ , 20 _00_ between

__Mickey Motivated Seller__ _____ the grantor, and

__Real Estate Solutions, Inc.__ _____ the grantee, whose address is

__Post Office Box 221, Denver, CO 80203__

WITNESSETH, that the grantor, for and in consideration of the sum of TEN DOLLARS ($10.00), the receipt and sufficiency of which is hereby acknowledged and received, and for other good and valuable consideration, has granted bargained, sold and conveyed, and by these presents does grant, bargain sell, convey and confirm unto the grantee, their heirs and assigns forever, all the real property, together with improvements, if any, situate and being in the County of _____ Denver _____ , State of ____ Colorado ____ , described as follows:

__Lot 21, Block 12, Brighton Subdivision #1, City & County of Denver__

Also known as street and number __123 Main Street, Denver, CO 80203__   .

TOGETHER with all and singular hereditaments and appurtenances thereunto belonging, or in anywise appertaining and the reversion and reversions, remainder and remainders, rents, issues, and profits thereof, and all the estate, right, title, interest, claim and demand whatsoever of the said grantor, either in law or equity, of, in and to the above bargained premises, with the hereditaments and appurtenances.

TO HAVE AND TO HOLD the said premises above bargained and described, with the appurtenances, unto the said grantee, their heirs and assigns forever. And the said grantor, for himself, his heirs, and personal representatives, does covenant, grant bargain and agree to and with the grantee, their heirs and assigns, that at the time of the ensealing and delivery of these presents, is well seized of the premises above conveyed, has good, sure, perfect, absolute indefeasible estate if inheritance, in law, in fee simple, and has good right, full power and lawful authority to grant, bargain, sell and convey the same in manner and form aforesaid, and that the same are free and clear from all former and other grants, bargains, sales, liens, taxes, assessments, encumbrances and restrictions of any kind or nature whatsoever, except any easements, restrictions, covenants, zoning ordinances and rights-of-way of record and property taxes accruing subsequent to __December 31, 1999__ , a lien not yet due and payable.

The grantor shall and will WARRANT AND FOREVER DEFEND the above-bargained premises in the quiet and peaceable possession of the grantee, his heirs, and assigns, against all and every person or persons lawfully claiming the whole or any part thereof. The singular shall include the plural, the plural shall include the singular, and the use of any gender shall be applicable to all genders.

IN WITNESS WHEREOF, the grantor has executed this deed on the date set forth above.

Mickey Motivated Seller
_____
Grantor

STATE OF __*Colorado*__ , COUNTY OF __*Denver*__)ss:

On __*Feb 1st*__ , 20 _*00*_ , before me, __*Nancy Notary*__ , a notary public in and for said state personally appeared
__*Mickey Motivated Seller*__   ,
_____ personally known to me (or proved to me based upon satisfactory evidence) to be the person(s) whose name(s) are subscribed to the within instrument and acknowledged that (s)he/they executed the same in his/her/their signature on the instrument the person(s) or entity on behalf of which they acted, executed the instrument.

Witness my hand and official seal

Nancy Notary
_____
NOTARY PUBLIC   My commission expires __*Jan 15, 2003*__

Recording requested by

and when recorded, please return this deed
and tax statements to:

Post Office Box 221, Denver, CO 80203

For recorder s use only

CALIFORNIA GRANT DEED

[   ] This transfer is exempt from the documentary transfer tax
[X] The documentary transfer tax is $_____ and is computed on:
     [   ] the full value of the interest in the property conveyed
     [X] the full value less the value of liens of encumbrances remaining at the time of sale
The property is located in an [   ] unincorporated area. [   ] the city of _Los Angeles_____

For a valuable consideration, receipt of which is hereby acknowledged,
Mickey Motivated Seller
hereby grant(s) to Real Estate Solutions, Inc.

the following real property in the City of _Los Angeles_____, County of _Los Angeles_,
_____state of California:

Lot 21, Block 4, Shady Acres 3rd Filing, City and County of Los
Angeles, State of California

Date: _____

           _____
           Grantor

Date: *Feb 1, 2000*

           *Mickey Motivated Seller*_____
           Grantor

STATE OF _*Colorado*____, COUNTY OF _*Denver*_____)ss:

On _*Feb 1st*____, 20_*00*_, before me, _*Nancy Notary*_____, a notary public in and for said state
personally appeared _*Mickey Motivated Seller*_____, personally known to me (or proved to me based
upon satisfactory evidence) to be the person(s) whose name(s) are subscribed to the within instrument and
acknowledged that (s)he/they executed the same in his/her/their signature on the instrument the person(s) or entity
on behalf of which they acted, executed the instrument.

Witness my hand and official seal

Nancy Notary
_____
NOTARY PUBLIC
My commission expires *Jan 15, 2003*

                                  [NOTARY SEAL]

Paul J. Piekos

Summary Appraisal Report
Property Description   **UNIFORM RESIDENTIAL APPRAISAL REPORT**   File No.   DEMO-URAR

SUBJECT		
Property Address 1234 White Eagle Drive	City Anywhere	State IL. Zip Code 605XX
Legal Description Lot X in White Eagle Club Unit X		County Will
Assessor's Parcel No. 01-04-101-XXX	Tax Year 1996 R.E. Taxes $ 7,564.32	Special Assessments $ 0.00
Borrower Buyn, Ima	Current Owner Seller, Homer	Occupant: ☒ Owner ☐ Tenant ☐ Vacant
Property rights appraised ☒ Fee Simple ☐ Leasehold	Project Type ☒ PUD ☐ Condominium (HUD/VA only)	HOA $ 65.00 /Mo.
Neighborhood or Project Name White Eagle Club	Map Reference 30W-10S	Census Tract 8803.02
Sale Price $ 425,000 Date of Sale 05/29/98	Description and $ amount of loan charges/concessions to be paid by seller None known	
Lender/Client XYZ Financial Inc.	Address 1234 Main Street, Anywhere, IL 605XX	
Appraiser Paul J. Piekos SRA	Address 413 Braemar Av., Naperville, IL 60563	

Location	☐ Urban ☒ Suburban ☐ Rural	**Predominant occupancy**	**Single family housing**	**Present land use %**	**Land use change**	
Built up	☒ Over 75% ☐ 25-75% ☐ Under 25%		PRICE $(000) / AGE (yrs)	One family 80	☐ Not likely ☐ Likely	
Growth rate	☒ Rapid ☐ Stable ☐ Slow	☒ Owner	180 Low 0	2-4 family	☒ In process	
Property values	☐ Increasing ☒ Stable ☐ Declining	☐ Tenant	700 High 10	Multi-family 5	To: Improved Resident	
Demand/supply	☐ Shortage ☒ In balance ☐ Over supply	☐ Vacant (0-5%)	Predominant	Commercial 10		
Marketing time	☐ Under 3 mos. ☒ 3-6 mos. ☐ Over 6 mos.	☐ Vac.(over 5%)	300 5	Industrial 5		

Note: Race and the racial composition of the neighborhood are not appraisal factors.

Neighborhood boundaries and characteristics: Predominantly single family detached housing. Boundaries are New York Street east, 95th Street south, Kendall County line west.

Factors that affect the marketability of the properties in the neighborhood (proximity to employment and amenities, employment stability, appeal to market, etc.): Subject is located in a rapidly growing area in a residential neighborhood comprised mostly of custom bui quality construction. Most all the dwellings appear to project good curb appeal. Compatibility of propert neighborhood services and conveniences are average for the area. Area employment has been stable and empl present or closeby. Overall, a marketable area with good appeal to purchasers within this price range.

Market conditions in the subject neighborhood (including support for the above conclusions related to the trend of property values, demand/supply, and marketing time -- such as data on competitive properties for sale in the neighborhood, description of the prevalence of sales and financing concessions, etc.): Housing values have either held steady or increased gradually within the past twelve months. Properties us The demand for housing in the subject neighborhood is consistent with the rest of nearby competing areas, under 90 days. Homes in the subject's price range have a typical marketing time of 90-120 days. Financing market rates. Financing is usually through the conventional process with the lower end of the value range concessions necessary.

Project Information for PUDs (If applicable) - - Is the developer/builder in control of the Home Owners' Association (HOA)?   ☒ Yes   ☐ No

Approximate total number of units in the subject project _____1100_____   Approximate total number of units for sale in the subject project _____59_____

Describe common elements and recreational facilities: Clubhouse, pool, tennis courts and the common areas.

SITE		
Dimensions 98 X 150 X 81 X 155		Topography Basically level
Site area Approx. 13,600 Sq.Ft.	Corner Lot ☐ Yes ☒ No	Size Typical for the area
Specific zoning classification and description R-1A P.U.D. Single Family Residential		Shape Slightly irregular
Zoning compliance ☒ Legal ☐ Legal nonconforming (Grandfathered use) ☐ Illegal ☐ No zoning		Drainage Appears adequate
Highest & best use as improved: ☒ Present use ☐ Other use (explain)		View Golf course

Utilities	Public	Other	Off-site Improvements	Type	Public	Private	
Electricity	☒	Underground	Street	Asphalt	☒	☐	Landscaping Good
Gas	☒		Curb/gutter	Concrete	☒	☐	Driveway Surface Concrete
Water	☒		Sidewalk	Concrete	☒	☐	Apparent easements Public utilities
Sanitary sewer	☒		Street lights	Electric	☒	☐	FEMA Special Flood Hazard Area ☐ Yes ☒ No
Storm sewer	☒		Alley	None			FEMA Zone Zone C Map Date 05/18/92
							FEMA Map No. #170213 0020C

Comments (apparent adverse easements, encroachments, special assessments, slide areas, illegal or legal nonconforming zoning use, etc.):   Site consists (average sized lot with a premium location that backs to the golf course which projects good appeal. Lands readily apparent adverse easements or encroachments.

DESCRIPTION OF IMPROVEMENTS					
GENERAL DESCRIPTION	EXTERIOR DESCRIPTION	FOUNDATION	BASEMENT	INSULATION	
No. of Units One	Foundation Poured Conc.	Slab None	Area Sq. Ft. 1,424	Roof	☐
No. of Stories Two	Exterior Walls Frame/Brick	Crawl Space Partial	% Finished 50%	Ceiling	☐
Type (Det./Att.) Detached	Roof Surface Asphalt Shin	Basement Partial	Ceiling Suspended	Walls	☐
Design (Style) 2 Story	Gutters & Dwnspts. Aluminum	Sump Pump Present	Walls Drywall	Floor	☐
Existing/Proposed Existing	Window Type Casement	Dampness None noted	Floor Carpeted	None	☐
Age (Yrs.) 4	Storm/Screens Thermalpane	Settlement None noted	Outside Entry None	Unknown Cncld.	☒
Effective Age (Yrs.) 2	Manufactured House No	Infestation None noted	200 amp service	Ceiling Fan(s)	

ROOMS	Foyer	Living	Dining	Kitchen	Den	Family Rm.	Rec. Rm.	Bedrooms	# Baths	Laundry	Other	Area Sq. Ft.
Basement							X					1,42
Level 1	X	1	1	1		1		1	1.5	X		2,26
Level 2								3	1.0			941

Finished area above grade contains: 8 Rooms;   4 Bedroom(s);   2.! Bath(s);   3,20 Square Feet of Gross Living Area

INTERIOR	Materials/Condition	HEATING		KITCHEN EQUIP.		ATTIC		AMENITIES		CAR STORAGE:	
Floors	Carpet/HW/Tile/G	Type	FWA	Refrigerator	☒	None	☐	Fireplace(s) # 1	☒	None	☐
Walls	Drywall/Good	Fuel	Gas	Range/Oven	☒	Stairs	☐	Patio Brick	☒	Garage # of cars	
Trim/Finish	Stained/Good	Condition	Good	Disposal	☒	Drop Stair	☐	Deck Wood	☒	Attached 3	
Bath Floor	Ceramic/Good	COOLING		Dishwasher	☒	Scuttle	☒	Porch	☐	Detached	
Bath Wainscot	Ceramic/Good	Central	Present	Fan/Hood	☒	Floor	☐	Fence	☐	Built-In	
Doors	Six Panel/Good	Other	None	Microwave	☐	Heated	☐	Pool Whirlpool T	☒	Carport	
Ceramic tile front entry		Condition	Good	Washer/Dryer	☒	Finished	☐	Skylights	☐	Driveway 6	

Additional features (special energy efficient items, etc.):   See attached addenda.

Condition of the improvements, depreciation (physical, functional, and external), repairs needed, quality of construction, remodeling/additions, etc.:   Subject property is in good condition, exhibiting minimal physical deterioration. Improvements are of very good q acceptable and considered typical for this style home in this area. No functional inadequacies or externa Marketability of the property is good.

Adverse environmental conditions (such as, but not limited to, hazardous wastes, toxic substances, etc.) present in the improvements, on the site, or in the immediate vicinity of the subject property.:   No visible external adverse environmental conditions were observed. No on-sit were disclosed to the appraiser at the time of inspection.

Freddie Mac Form 70 6/93	PAGE 1 OF 2	Fannie Mae Form 1004 6/93

Form UA2   "TOTAL 2000 for Windows" appraisal software by a la mode, inc.   1-800-ALAMODE

File No. DEMO-URAR | Page #3

UNIFORM RESIDENTIAL APPRAISAL REPORT

File No. DEMO-URAR

Valuation Section

COST APPROACH

ESTIMATED SITE VALUE .... = $ 100,00

ESTIMATED REPRODUCTION COST-NEW-OF IMPROVEMENTS:

Dwelling	3,20 Sq. Ft. @$ 81.35	= $	260,40
Appliances, FP, Whirlpool, Deck	1,42 Sq. Ft. @$ 37.04	=	52,74
			24,10
Garage/Carport 774 Sq. Ft. @$ 29.93	=		23,16
Total Estimated Cost New	.... = $		360,41
Less	Physical	Functional	External
Depreciation 10,30	0	0	= $ 10,30
Depreciated Value of Improvements	.... = $		350,11
"As-is" Value of Site Improvements	.... = $		7,07
INDICATED VALUE BY COST APPROACH	.... = $		457,18

Comments on Cost Approach (such as, source of cost estimate, site value, square foot calculation and for HUD, VA and FmHA, the estimated remaining economic life of the property): Physical depreciation is calc using the effective age/economic life method on No significant functional obsolescence or exter was observed. Due to the lack of available vacar the allocation method was used to estimate the s is replacement cost. Figures taken from the Mar Residential Cost Handbook for a single family dw good quality construction. Estimated remaining e 68 years.

SALES COMPARISON ANALYSIS

ITEM	SUBJECT	COMPARABLE NO. 1		COMPARABLE NO. 2		COMPARABLE NO. 3	
Address	1234 White Eagle Drive Anywhere	3607 Scottsdale Circle Anywhere		3123 Aviara Circle Anywhere		3131 Aviara Circle Anywhere	
Proximity to Subject		2 Blocks South		3 Blocks East		3 Blocks East	
Sales Price	$ 425,00		$ 418,00		$ 444,50		$ 453,00
Price/Gross Living Area	$ 132.7	$ 123.8		$ 121.4		$ 111.6	
Data and/or Verification Source	Inspection Assessor	MLS of Northern Illinois Wheatland Twsp. Assessor		MLS of Northern Illinois Wheatland Twsp. Assessor		MLS of Northern Illinois Wheatland Twsp. Assessor	
VALUE ADJUSTMENTS	DESCRIPTION	DESCRIPTION	+( )$ Adjust.	DESCRIPTION	+( )$ Adjust.	DESCRIPTION	+( )$ Adjust.
Sales or Financing Concessions		Conventional None Known		Conventional None Known		Conventional None Known	
Date of Sale/Time		11/97		2/98		7/97	
Location	Good	Similar		Similar		Similar	
Leasehold/Fee Simple	Fee Simple	Fee Simple		Fee Simple		Fee Simple	
Site	98 X 150 irre	70 X 151 irre	+10,00	119 X 150 irr		90 X 135 irre	
View	Golf Course	Golf Course		Golf Course		Golf Course	
Design and Appeal	2 Story/Good	2 Story/Equal		2 Story/Equal		2 Story/Equal	
Quality of Construction	Frame/Brick	Dryvit/Stone		Frame/Brick		Frame/Brick	
Age	4	2		2		3	
Condition	Good	Good		Good		Good	
Above Grade Room Count	Total 8 : Bdrms 4 : Baths 2.5	Total 10 : Bdrms 3 : Baths 3.5	-2,00	Total 9 : Bdrms 4 : Baths 4.0	-3,00	Total 10 : Bdrms 4 : Baths 4.0	-3,00
Gross Living Area	3,20 Sq. Ft.	3,37 Sq. Ft.	-6,96	3,66 Sq. Ft.	-18,36	4,05 Sq. Ft.	-34,20
Basement & Finished Rooms Below Grade	Partial 50% Finished	Partial None	+10,00	Partial None	+10,00	Partial None	+10,00
Functional Utility	Average	Average		Average		Average	
Heating/Cooling	GFWA/CAC	GFWA/CAC		GFWA/CAC		GFWA/CAC	
Energy Efficient Items	Skylights	Skylights		Skylights		Skylights	
Garage/Carport	3 Car Garage	3 Car Garage		3 Car Garage		3 Car Garage	
Porch, Patio, Deck, Fireplace(s), etc.	Deck, Patio 1 Fireplace	Deck, Patio 1 Fireplace		Deck 2 Fireplaces	+2,00 -2,50	Deck 1 Fireplace	+2,00
Fence, Pool, etc.	Whirlpool Tub	Whirlpool Tub		Whirlpool Tub		Whirlpool Tub	
Other	Security Syst	Security Syst		Security Syst		Security Syst	
Net Adj. (total)		☒ +	11,04	+ ☐	11,86	+ ☒	25,20
Adjusted Sales Price of Comparable		Net 2.6 % Gross 6.9 %	429,04	Net 2.7 % Gross 8.1 %	432,64	Net 5.6 % Gross 10.9 %	427,80

Comments on Sales Comparison (including the subject property's compatibility to the neighborhood, etc.): All sales are similar custom built hom the subject subdivision. Comps #2 and #3 are located in a similar phase of the subject subdivision, Comp the lot sizes are smaller. All have similar locations that back to the golf course. All were adjusted for homes adjusted for size @ $40 per sq.ft. All lack the finished basement. All have similar amenities to th over six months old, it was the best available. A time adjustment is not necessary. Most weight was given from Comp #1.

ITEM	SUBJECT	COMPARABLE NO. 1	COMPARABLE NO. 2	COMPARABLE NO. 3
Date, Price and Data Source, for prior sales within year of appraisal	No prior sale the past 12 months per ML	No other prior sale repo the past 12 months per M public records and/or as	No other prior sale repo the past 12 months per M public records and/or as	No other prior sale repo the past 12 months per M public records and/or as

Analysis of any current agreement of sale, option, or listing of subject property and analysis of any prior sales of subject and comparables within one year of the date of appraisal: Subject property sold within 95% of the list price and within a reasonable marketing time for similar lik comparable sales used shows no other recent sales activity.

INDICATED VALUE BY SALES COMPARISON APPROACH .... $ 429,00

INDICATED VALUE BY INCOME APPROACH (if Applicable) Estimated Market Rent $ N/A /Mo. x Gross Rent Multiplier N/A = $ N/A

This appraisal is made ☒ "as is" ☐ subject to the repairs, alterations, inspections or conditions listed below ☐ subject to completion per plans & specifications.

Conditions of Appraisal: Personal property items were not considered in the valuation of the real property.

Final Reconciliation: While the cost approach indicates a higher value, the sales comparison approach was given the in the final conclusion. As this type of property is typically owner-occupied, the income approach has ins

RECONCILIATION

The purpose of this appraisal is to estimate the market value of the real property that is the subject of this report, based on the above conditions and the certification, contingent and limiting conditions, and market value definition that are stated in the attached Freddie Mac Form 439/FNMA form 1004B (Revised 6/93).

I (WE) ESTIMATE THE MARKET VALUE, AS DEFINED, OF THE REAL PROPERTY THAT IS THE SUBJECT OF THIS REPORT, AS OF June 2, 1998 (WHICH IS THE DATE OF INSPECTION AND THE EFFECTIVE DATE OF THIS REPORT) TO BE $ 429,000

APPRAISER:

Signature *Paul J. Piekos*

Name Paul J. Piekos SRA

Date Report Signed June 2, 1998

State Certification # 156-XXXXXX State IL

Or State License #

SUPERVISORY APPRAISER (ONLY IF REQUIRED):

Signature

Name

Date Report Signed

State Certification #

Or State License #

☐ Did ☐ Did Not Inspect Property

State

State

Freddie Mac Form 70 6/93

PAGE 2 OF 2

Fannie Mae Form 1004 6-93

Form UA2 "TOTAL 2000 for Windows" appraisal software by a la mode, inc. 1-800-ALAMODE

INDEPENDENT CONTRACTOR AGREEMENT

AGREEMENT made this <u>1st</u> day of <u>Feb</u>, 20 <u>00</u> by and between <u>Real Estate Solutions, :</u> (hereinafter "Corporation") whose address is <u>Post Office Box 221, Denver, CO 80203</u> and <u>Carl Contractor</u>
_____ , whose address is _____
<u>234 Havana St, Aurora, CO 80011</u> (hereinafter "Contractor").

SERVICES TO BE PERFORMED

Contractor agrees to perform the following services for Corporation:

<u>Repair drywall in kitchen and living room; paint bathroom</u>

PLACE OF PERFORMANCE

The work described above shall be performed at:_____
<u>123 Main Street, Denver, CO 80203</u>

TIME PERIOD

Contractor agrees to commence work as soon as practical and complete all work by <u>Feb 12th</u>, 20 <u>00</u>. Contractor agrees to subtract $<u>50.00</u> per day for each day the work is not completed as liquidated damages and not as a penalty from the total bill of services performed.

PAYMENT FOR SERVICES

Contractor shall be paid not by the hour or the day, but upon complete of certain repairs as follows: <u>1,000 upon completion of drywall 1/2 fee, balance after painting completed</u>

SUPERVISION

Corporation shall not supervise or directly control the work of Contractor. Corporation does reserve the right, from time to time, to inspect the work being performed to determine whether it is being performed in a good and "workmanlike" manner. Contractor shall have the ultimate authority to determine the hours of work, the length of workdays, the means and methods of performance of the work, and Corporation shall not interfere in this regard.

MATERIALS

Contractor will obtain and provide all necessary materials for the services described above at his own expense.

INVOICES

Contractor agrees to provide Corporation with written invoices for all work performed.

SUBCONTRACTORS OR ASSISTANTS

Contractor may, in his discretion and at his own expense, employ such assistants or subcontractors as may be necessary for the performance of work. Contractor agrees to pay any wages, taxes, unemployment insurance, withholding taxes, workers compensation insurance required by law for assistants or subcontractors. Said assistants or subcontractors will not be paid or supervised by Corporation.

EQUIPMENT

Contractor agrees to provide his own equipment or tools for the work to be performed.

INSURANCE

Contractor agrees to provide his own liability insurance for work performed, naming Corporation as additional insured. In the event that Contractor does not maintain insurance, he shall defend and indemnify Corporation for all lawsuits, accidents or claims arising out of his work, or the work of his assistants or subcontractors.

INDEPENDENT CONTRACTOR

Contractor agrees that he is completely independent from Corporation and is not an employee of Corporation. Contractor warrants that he may, and in fact does work for other individuals and/or entities.

	Real Estate Solutions, Inc.
Carl Contractor	*by Ira Investor, president*
Contractor	Corporation

JOINT VENTURE AGREEMENT

THIS JOINT VENTURE AGREEMENT (the "Agreement"), made and entered into as of this ___1st___ day of ____Feb____ , 20_00_ by and between _Real Estate Solutions, Inc._ and _Anton Investor_ .

1. BUSINESS PURPOSE:

The business of the Joint Venture shall be to purchase certain real estate located at _123 Main Street, Denver, CO 80203_ in the County of ____Denver____ , State of _____Colorado_____ for the purpose of renovation and sale for profit.

2. TERM OF THE AGREEMENT:

This Joint Venture shall commence on the date first above written and shall continue in existence until terminated, liquidated, or dissolved by law or as hereinafter provided.

3. OBLIGATIONS OF THE JOINT VENTURERS:

[Set forth in detail the obligations of the parties, for example, who will contribute cash, property and other services, who will pay workers, who will supervise the project, who will contribute money for cost overruns, etc]

4. PROFITS AND LOSSES:

Upon the sale of the property and receipt of all proceeds therefrom, the parties will be reimbursed their actual, out of pocket expenses directed related to the Venture. After all expenses, debts and costs related to the Venture and the property, the parties agree to split the Net Proceeds as follows:

Anton Investor shall receive _50_ %

Real Estate Solutions, Inc shall receive _50_ %

5. <u>INDEMNIFICATION OF THE JOINT VENTURERS</u>:

The parties to this Agreement shall have no liability to the other for any loss suffered which arises out of any action or inaction if, in good faith, it is determined that such course of conduct was in the best interests of the Joint Venture and such course of conduct did not constitute negligence or misconduct. The parties to this Agreement shall each be indemnified by the other against losses, judgments, liabilities, expenses and amounts paid in settlement of any claims sustained by it in connection with the Joint Venture.

6. <u>DISSOLUTION</u>:

The Joint Venture shall be dissolved upon the happening of any of the following events:

(a) The adjudication of bankruptcy, filing of a petition pursuant to a Chapter of the Federal Bankruptcy Act, withdrawal, removal or insolvency of either of the parties.

(b) The sale or other disposition, not including an exchange of all, or substantially all, of the Joint Venture assets.

(c) Mutual agreement of the parties.

7. <u>COMPLETE AGREEMENT</u>:

This Agreement constitutes the full and complete understanding and agreement of the parties hereto with respect to the subject matter hereof, and there are no agreements, understandings, restrictions or warranties among the parties other than those set forth herein provided for.

8. <u>UNIFORM PARTNERSHIP ACT</u>

Anything not specifically set forth herein shall be governed by the applicable rules of the Uniform Partnership Act of the State of ____Colorado_____.

IN WITNESS WHEREOF, the parties hereto have executed this Agreement as of the day and year first above written. Signed, sealed and delivered in the presence of:

*Anton Investor*_____
Joint Venturer

Real Estate Solutions, Inc.
*by Ira Investor, president*_____
Joint Venturer

State-by-State Foreclosure Guide

The following is a summary of foreclosure laws and practices for all 50 states and the District of Columbia. This information is merely a summary and is not intended as a substitute for sound legal counsel. The information is divided into five columns:

- *State.* The state in which you are looking for foreclosure properties
- *Type of Security Most Commonly Used.* Although both deeds of trust and mortgages are available as collateral for a real estate loan, most lenders use one or the other exclusively in each state.
- *Foreclosure Method.* The legal method by which the lender seeks to liquidate the collateral to recoup its funds.
- *Redemption Period.* The amount of time, if any, a borrower has after the foreclosure sale date to come up with funds to keep the property.
- *Misc.* Other information, such as a legal right a borrower has to reinstate the loan rather than pay it off in full.

STATE	TYPE OF SECURITY MOST COMMONLY USED	FORECLOSURE METHOD	REDEMPTION PERIOD	MISC
Alabama	Mortgage	Power of Sale	12 months	Borrower can reinstate his loan within 5 days of sale
Alaska	Deed of Trust	Power of Sale	None	Borrower can reinstate loan up to date of sale so long as a notice of defaulted has not been filed more than 2x in the past
Arizona	Mortgage	Judicial	None	
Arkansas	Deed of Trust	Power of Sale	Within one year	
California	Deed of Trust	Power of Sale	None	
Colorado	Deed of Trust	Power of Sale	75 days	Borrower can cure up to sale date
Connecticut	Mortgage	Strict Foreclosure	None, unless ordered by the court	A strict foreclosure vests title in the lender without a sale. Borrower cannot reinstate the loan. A court may delay the foreclosure for up to six months if the borrower is not making enough money!
Delaware	Mortgage	Judicial	None	
Dist. Of Columbia	Deed of Trust	Power of Sale	None	Borrower can reinstate up to 45 days before sale once in two consecutive years
Florida	Mortgage	Judicial	Up to the date the clerk files the certificate of sale	
Georgia	Mortgage	Power of Sale	None	
Hawaii	Mortgage	Power of Sale	None	
Idaho	Deed of Trust	Power of Sale	None	Borrower can cure with 115 days of the filing of the notice of default
Illinois	Mortgage	Judicial	Until the latter of 3 months of entry of judgment or 7 months of service of the foreclosure complaint	Borrower has 90 days from the service of the complaint to reinstate
Indiana	Mortgage	Judicial	None	
Iowa	Mortgage	Judicial	One year	
Kansas	Mortgage	Judicial	3-12 months, depending on the property's equity	
Kentucky	Mortgage & Deed of Trust	Judicial	Up to one year if the sale does not bring at least 2/3 of the property's value	
Louisiana	Mortgage	Judicial	None	
Maine	Mortgage	Judicial	Within one year unless the mortgage agreement provides for less	Borrower can reinstate within 30 days of default
Maryland	Deed of Trust	Power of Sale with court supervision	None stated, although equitable redemption permitted	
Massachusetts	Mortgage	Power of Sale	None	
Michigan	Mortgage	Power of Sale	Varies, but generally 6 months on houses	
Minnesota	Mortgage	Power of Sale	6 to 12 months, depending on equity	
Mississippi	Deed of Trust	Power of Sale	None	Borrower can reinstate up to the date of sale
Missouri	Deed of Trust	Power of Sale	One year if the lender purchases the property at sale	
Montana	Deed of Trust	Judicial	None	
Nebraska	Deed of Trust	Judicial	None	Borrower can reinstate before sale
Nevada	Deed of Trust	Power of Sale	None	Borrower has 35 days from filing of notice of default to reinstate loan
New Hampshire	Mortgage	Power of Sale	None	NH mortgage can also have a strict foreclosure provision
New Jersey	Mortgage	Judicial	6 months after entry of judgment	
New Mexico	Mortgage	Judicial	9 months, but may be as little as 1 month by agreement in writing	
New York	Mortgage	Judicial	None	
North Carolina	Deed of Trust	Power of Sale	None	
North Dakota	North Dakota	Judicial	One year	
Ohio	Mortgage	Judicial	Only up to the date of confirmation of sale	
Oklahoma	Mortgage	Judicial	Only up to the date of confirmation of sale	
Oregon	Deed of Trust	Power of Sale	None	Borrower may reinstate up to 5 days before sale
Pennsylvania	Mortgage	Judicial	None	Borrower may reinstate before the sale, up to 3x in 1 year
Rhode Island	Mortgage	Power of Sale	Up to 3 years by filing a lawsuit	
South Carolina	Mortgage	Judicial	None	
South Dakota	Mortgage	Power of Sale	None	Borrower can make lender go through a judicial foreclosure
Tennessee	Deed of Trust	Power of Sale	Up to 2 years	
Texas	Deed of Trust	Power of Sale	None	Borrower has 20 days from notice of default to reinstate loan
Utah	Deed of Trust	Judicial	6 months	Borrower can reinstate within 3 months of notice of default
Vermont	Mortgage	Strict Foreclosure	None	
Virginia	Deed of Trust	Power of Sale	None	
Washington	Deed of Trust	Power of Sale	None	Borrower can reinstate loan up to 11 days before sale
West Virginia	Deed of Trust	Power of Sale	None if the sale is confirmed by the court	Borrower has 10 days from notice of default to reinstate loan
Wisconsin	Mortgage	Judicial	None	Borrower has until sale date to cure default
Wyoming	Mortgage	Power of Sale	None	

LOCAL FORECLOSURE INFORMATION PROVIDERS

List provided courtesy of Foreclosures.com.

Alabama
Courthouse Retrieval
423-584-8017

Arizona
Foreclosure Listings of Arizona, Inc. (Maricopa County)
800-310-7730

California
Daily Default Infoservice (San Francisco Bay and Sacramento Valley areas)
800-310-7730

County Records Service and Foreclosures.com (San Diego County)
800-310-7730

County Records Research and Foreclosures.com (Los Angeles, San Bernardino, Riverside, and Orange County areas)
800-310-7730

Colorado
Property Data Center
303-850-9576

Connecticut
Connecticut Foreclosure Alert
860-345-2100

Florida
Foreclosure Reporting Service (Covering South Florida)
954-964-3435

Jacksonville Daily Record
904-356-2466

Georgia
REIS
800-633-6708

Market Data Center
770-246-4545

Illinois
Foreclosure Report of Chicago (6 Chicagoland counties)
800-310-7730

Maine
Foreclosure Report
847-842-9200

Maryland
Specprint
410-561-9600

Massachusetts
Foreclosure Report
888-297-3343

Minnesota
Moore Data Management
612-588-7116

Nevada

Foreclosure Listings of Nevada
623-842-2755

New Hampshire

Real Data Corp
800-639-3282

Foreclosure Report
888-297-3343

New Jersey

All 21 counties by njlispendens.com
800-758-1236

New York

Profiles Publications Inc. and Foreclosures.com (Bronx, Brooklyn, Manhattan, and Queens)
800-310-7730

Long Island Profiles (Nassau and Suffolk counties)
631-968-8833

North Carolina

Courthouse Retrieval
423-584-8017

REO ~ USA
919-755-1101
877-473-6872

Ohio

The Foreclosure Newsletter
614-882-0198

Cincinnati Court Index
513-241-1450

Oklahoma

Foreclosure Research Service (Tulsa County)
918-437-8307

Pennsylvania

Realist
215-925-5400

Rhode Island

Foreclosure Report
888-297-3343

South Carolina

REIS
800-633-6708

Courthouse Retrieval
423-584-8017

Tennessee

Chandler & Chandler
901-458-6419

Courthouse Retrieval
423-584-8017

Texas

Foreclosure Listing Service, Inc. (Dallas and Ft. Worth)
972-250-0993

Foreclosure Listing Service
281-363-2631

Utah

Intermountain Record
801-972-5642

Vermont

Real Data Corp
800-639-3282

Virginia

ISC Information Services Corp.
305-262-6236

BisRE.com
800-683-0196

Washington

Northwest Foreclosures (King, Pierce, Snohomish counties)
800-530-RENS

Investor's Edge (King, Pierce, Snohomish counties)
425-827-4545

Wisconsin

MidWest Foreclosures (Milwaukee)
847-842-9200

Internet Resources

HOME SALE INFORMATION ONLINE (FREE SERVICES)

- *Yahoo! Home Values.* <realestate.yahoo.com/realestate/homevalues/address.html>
- *The Real Estate Center.* <recenter.tamu.edu/links/> Links to county tax assessor offices across the country for public information about property sales
- *HomePriceCheck.com.* Free online information on home sales in 27 states

FORECLOSURE LISTINGS (SOME FREE, SOME FEE BASED)

- *Federal Real Estate Loans and Mortgages.* <www.federalrealestate.net> Information about credit reporting, foreclosed homes, government and bank-owned properties

- *Department of Housing and Urban Development*. <www. hud.gov> Information by area of HUD repos for sale
- *Foreclosures.com*. Online foreclosure lists and educational information
- *Foreclosures-usa.com*. Another foreclosure reporting service, including IRS/GSA properties
- *e4close.com*. Free list of foreclosures, REOs, and government properties

REAL ESTATE DATA INFORMATION SERVICES (FEE BASED)

- *Dataquick*. <www.dataquick.com>
- *First American Information Services*. <www.firstamres.com/html/index.html>

OTHER INTERNET REAL ESTATE RESOURCES

- *Legalwiz.com*. Your resource for legal and small business information
- *Creative Real Estate Online*. <www.creonline.com> Meeting place for real estate investors from beginner to advanced
- *RealEstateLink.net*. Another network of real estate investors sharing ideas
- *Realestatinvesting.com*. A state-by-state network of real estate investing resources

Index